THE KIDS WINTER HANDBOOK

BY JANE DRAKE & ANN LOVE
ILLUSTRATED BY HEATHER COLLINS

KIDS CAN PRESS

Kids Can Press acknowledges the financial support of the Government of Canada, through the BPIDP, for our publishing activity.

Published in Canada by
Kids Can Press Ltd.
29 Birch Avenue
Toronto, ON M4V 1E2

Published in the U.S. by
Kids Can Press Ltd.
2250 Military Road
Tonawanda, NY 14150

www.kidscanpress.com

Edited by Laurie Wark
Designed by Blair Kerrigan/Glyphics
Printed and bound in Canada

US 01 0 9 8 7 6 5 4 3 2 1
US PA 01 0 9 8 7 6 5 4 3 2 1

Canadian Cataloguing in Publication Data

Drake, Jane
        The kids winter handbook

Includes index.
ISBN 1-55337-033-3 (bound) - ISBN 1-55074-969-2 (pbk.)

        1. Amusements — Juvenile literature. 2. Outdoor recreation — Juvenile literature. 3. Winter — Juvenile literature. I. Collins, Heather II. Love, Ann III. Title.

GV1203.D73 2001a   j790.1'922   C2001-900531-8

Kids Can Press is a Nelvana company

ACKNOWLEDGMENTS

The authors wish to acknowledge the contribution to this book of the following people: Ruth Andrews; Doreen Barnett; Fran and Will Barnett; Judy and Ian Barnett; Kathleen and Henry Barnett; Patrick Barnett; Betsy Bascom; Linda Biesenthal; Minnie Bloem; Julie Booker; Cathi Bremner; Trish Brooks; Bob Bryan; Jane Crist; Janet Dobson; Jim, Stephanie, Brian and Madeline Drake; Ruth Drake; Stephen and Martha Drake; Nicky Dummett; Pete and Maddy Ewins; Muriel and Ellsworth Flavelle; Dave Gibson; George and Gilbert Flowers; Millie Gourlay; Frank Gomes; Bob Graham; Jeanne Field; Wendy Fletcher; Margaret Stockwell Hart; Ryan Hennessey; Matt and June Heron; Richard Hodge; Heather Irwin; Colleen Jones; Lynn Kestle; Kingcrafts; Jackie Hilton; Sue Leppington; Mary Ann and Rob Lewis; Betty and Gage Love; David, Melanie, Jennifer and Adrian Love; Gage, Peter and Geoff Love; Scott Marshall; Murray McDonald; Mimi McEvenue; Blair McLorie; Rhea Morris; Donna O'Connor; Maria and Steven Price; Steve Pugh; Luke Racine; Wendy Reifel; Hilary Robinson; Robert Ross; Mari Rutka; Mark Salmoni; Alex Sharpe; Angus Sidney; Steph Smith; Elianna Stein; Shelley Steinman; Doug Stewart; Mary Thompson; Derek and Kelly Totten; Margaret Wedd; Richard Willan and Howard Wood.

Thanks to Valerie Hussey and all the people at Kids Can Press. A special thanks to our editor, Laurie Wark, who obviously knows how to have fun.

This book is dedicated to Kay Barnett,
whose soup and stories always warm our winters.

CONTENTS

INDOOR WINTER FUN

CELEBRATE WINTER

WELCOME WINTER

You'll always have fun in winter when you know what to expect and how to outwit the cold. In this section, you'll find out how to forecast the weather and spot special effects in the winter sky.

You'll also learn how to knit a cozy hat or sew a neckwarmer to wear while you look for winter constellations and the northern lights. Then carry wood indoors using your custom-made log carrier and warm up in front of the fire with stories and a cup of homemade soup.

There are lots of ways to beat the cold and enjoy wintertime.

WILD WEATHER

Will winter bring frosty mornings with piles of snow? Or will it stay mild and green outside? Some people say they can forecast winter weather by observing wildlife in the fall. Check this list of plant and animal lore to decide what kind of winter is in store for you.

If you notice these signs in the fall, winter may be cold, severe and long:

Deer grow extra thick fur and squirrels' tails grow more bushy.

The hair of wooly bear caterpillars grows so the black stripes are wider than the brown ones.

Onion skins grow unusually thick.

Muskrats build new houses.

Rose bushes bend over, heavy with rosehips.

8

Squirrels and chipmunks are extra busy storing their piles of nuts and seeds.

The tops of spruce and pine trees have a lot of cones.

Beavers build their winter lodges unusually early.

GROUNDHOG DAY

In North America, the most famous wild weather forecaster is the groundhog. The story goes that if a groundhog can see its shadow on the morning of February 2, there will be six more weeks of winter. But if it sees no shadow, spring is just around the corner. When sleepy groundhogs hibernate right through February 2, people look for their own shadows to make the prediction.

WINTER WEATHER RECORDS

- The coldest spot on earth is Plateau Station, Antarctica, where the average yearly temperature is -56.7°C (-70.1°F)!

- Silver City, Colorado, holds the world's record for the greatest snowfall in 24 hours: 195 cm (76 in.). Bessans, France, comes a close second with 173 cm (68 in.) of fresh snow in 19 hours.

9

WINDSOCK FORECASTING

You'll be the best winter forecaster around if you make this windsock to measure the wind's direction and strength.

You'll need:
a ³⁄₄ m (2 ft.) stick or wood dowel, 1 cm (¹⁄₂ in.) thick
a 2 cm (³⁄₄ in.) wood screw and screwdriver
needle-nosed pliers
75 cm (2¹⁄₂ ft.) wire from a coat hanger
scissors
a 1 m x 1 m (3 ft. x 3 ft.) square of nylon fabric
a needle and thread

1.

Screw the wood screw partway into one end of the stick so the screw head sticks out about 1 cm (¹⁄₂ in.).

2.

With the pliers, twist one end of the wire into a small, loose loop around the stick about 15 cm (6 in.) below the screw.

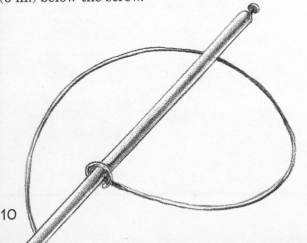

3.

With the pliers, bend the next 30 cm (1 ft.) of wire into an arc from the loop up to the screw neck.

4.

Make a second loop around the screw, loose enough to turn on the neck but tight enough not to slip off the head.

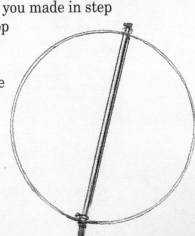

5.

Bend the remaining wire into another arc back down to your starting point to complete a wire circle with the arc you made in step 3. Make a final loop around the stick below your first loop. You should be able to hold the stick and swing the wire frame around it.

6.

Fold the nylon square in half, good side facing in. Center the wire frame on the nylon at one end of the folded fabric. Cut through both pieces of nylon to make identical triangles that are wider than the wire frame at one end and then taper to a point (or tail) at the other.

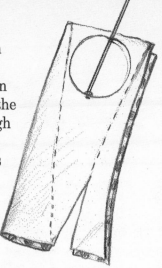

7.

Sew the long sides of the triangles together. Tie off the sewing on each side just before the ends to leave a small hole in the tail of the sock.

8.

Turn the sock right side out. Pull the wide mouth end of the sock into the frame and fold 5 cm (2 in.) of the nylon back over the wire. Fold again to make a hem and stitch the sock onto the frame so it swings easily.

9.

With the help of an adult, mount the windsock by wiring or nailing the stick on the top of a pole or roof. The sock should spin freely.

USING YOUR WINDSOCK

A windsock swivels so the mouth always faces the wind. Strong winds will fill the whole sock, lifting the tail end to the level of the mouth. Watch your windsock in winter. Decide from which direction fair-weather winds blow and how high the tail usually lifts. Then, when you see wind from another direction and with a different strength, expect a weather change.

Because winter weather often moves in huge circling systems, you can use "the crosswinds rule" to forecast. If you see high clouds moving in a direction that cuts across the wind in your windsock, stand facing the mouth of your windsock, the wind at your back. If the high clouds are moving from your left, poor weather is usually coming; but if the clouds are moving from your right, fair weather is on the way.

WINTER SUN

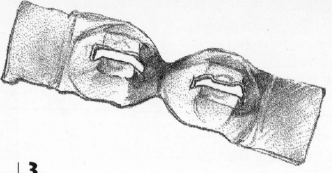

Early arctic people invented snow goggles to protect their eyes from the intense glare of the sun bouncing off snow. Make your own snow goggles and see what a difference they make.

You'll need:
scissors or a craft knife
a cardboard egg carton
2 pieces of string, each 50 cm (20 in.) long

1.
Cut two cups from the egg carton so that they are attached to each other and to the flaps of cardboard on the outer side of each cup.

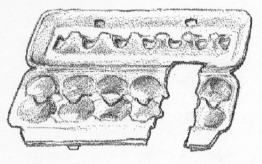

2.
Trim the cardboard bridge between the two cups until the goggles fit comfortably against your nose and brow.

3.
Cut a 0.5 cm (1/4 in.) slit across the bottom and a little way up the sides of each cup. Place the goggles on your eyes and decide if you need to widen or lengthen the slits so that you can see well straight ahead and side to side.

4.
Poke a hole in each side flap and attach the strings so you can tie on the goggles at the back of your head.

5.
On a sunny day, test your goggles. Don't wear them near traffic or in places where you need to take care as you walk or climb. **Never stare right at the sun.**

THE SUN'S SPECIAL EFFECTS

The North Pole tilts away from the sun in winter. That makes winter days north of the Equator shorter. Sunshine that does reach the north comes in at an angle, from the southern sky. With fewer hours of sun and with less direct sun, northern lands cool down. But winter sun, because it is weaker and shining from afar, can make amazing special effects in the skies. Look for sun dogs, sun haloes and sun pillars.

Sun dogs appear when the sun is low in the sky. They look like mini-suns that sit beside the sun. A sun dog is an image of the sun made by ice crystals in the air. When two sun dogs line up on either side of the sun, a sun halo may connect them to a huge arcing circle over the sun. A sun pillar is a beam of light that shines up from the rising or setting sun like a giant searchlight. The sun's rays have to hit six-sided ice crystals in a certain way to make this effect.

THE NIGHT SKY

On clear, crisp evenings, the winter sky can be brilliant with flaming meteors, the northern lights or a shining moon. Bundle up in layers so you can lie down on the snow and sky-gaze.

METEOR SHOWERS

Some people call meteors "falling stars," but meteors are not stars. They are microscopic flecks of space dust or debris that flare up and vaporize when they hit Earth's atmosphere. Twice a winter, on December 13 and January 4, Earth passes through unusually thick trails of debris left by comets. On those nights, you can see up to 80 meteors an hour in sensational meteor showers. The show is best after midnight when you see the tails rather than the heads of the meteors.

14

NORTHERN LIGHTS

Northern lights usually start as a pale green glow in the north. The glow can brighten, widen and then separate into distinct, up and down spikes. In spectacular displays, the spikes line up so that they look like folds on giant curtains that seem to waver side to side and shimmer red, blue, yellow and green. Some people say they even make a crackling sound.

Scientists say they are high-energy particles released from the sun that burst into color when they hit the upper atmosphere over Earth's magnetic poles.

WINTER MOON

A full moon on a crisp winter night can be so bright that shadows form on the snow below.

When you see a tiny crescent moon in winter, look carefully. Beside the bright sliver, you may see the whole face of the moon lit in a pale light. People say "the old moon is in the new moon's arms." In winter, the moon and the Earth line up in such a way that sunlight reflects off Earth and onto the darkened face of the moon. The moon is lit with "earthshine."

WINTER STARS

Take the star map (page 17) outside after dark and find a place where the whole sky is in view. Look north and hold the map in front of you with the word "North" at the bottom of the map. Or look south and hold the map with the word "South" at the bottom. Wear a pair of red mitts and tuck a flashlight inside one mitt. The light will keep your hand warm and the red glow will allow you to read the star chart in the dark and still see the stars above.

THE BIG DIPPER, THE NORTH STAR AND THE GREAT BEAR

Look north to find the seven stars that form a long-handled pot, the Big Dipper. Follow where water would pour from the Dipper to find the North Star. The Big Dipper forms part of the Great Bear, a group of stars the ancient Greeks called *arcticos* from which we get our word "Arctic."

ORION THE HUNTER, TAURUS THE BULL AND CANIS THE DOG

Look south to find the three stars of Orion's belt. Orion has bright stars for his shoulders and knees and fainter stars for his sword. Find the fuzzy nebula, or gas and dust cloud, in the middle of his sword. Orion the hunter fights the charging bull, Taurus. Following on Orion's heels is his dog, Canis, whose eye is the brightest star in the sky.

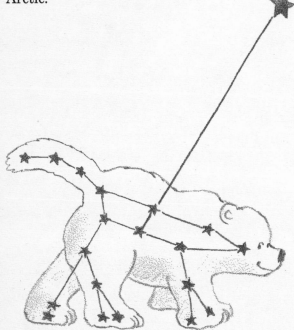

NORTH

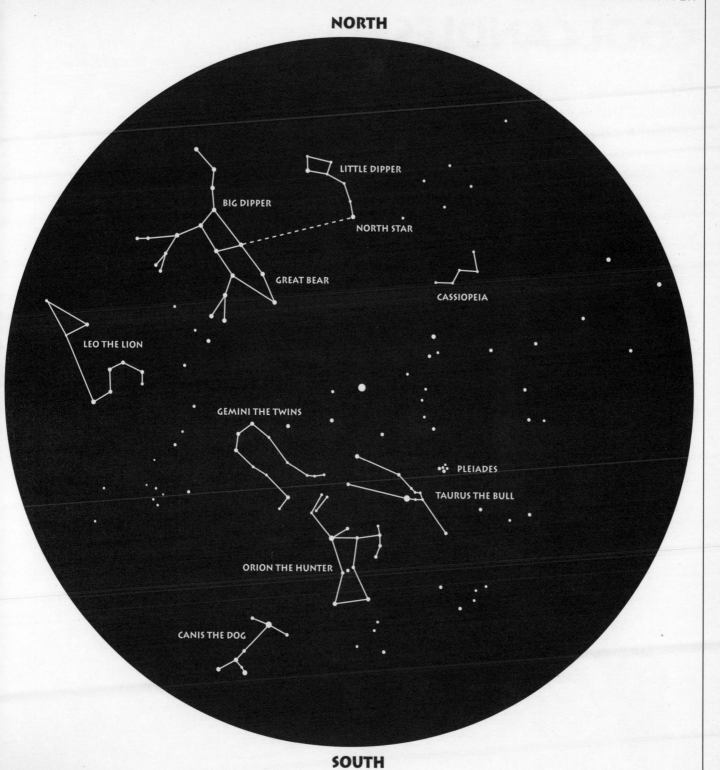

LITTLE DIPPER

BIG DIPPER

NORTH STAR

GREAT BEAR

CASSIOPEIA

LEO THE LION

GEMINI THE TWINS

PLEIADES

TAURUS THE BULL

ORION THE HUNTER

CANIS THE DOG

SOUTH

COOL CANDLES

Bring the ice indoors with the frosty glitter of this icy candleholder. Make several for a sensational display.

You'll need:
Plasticine or other modeling clay
a clean empty coffee can
water
a tea-candle
a saucer

1.

Push a golf ball-sized piece of Plasticine firmly into the bottom of the coffee can.

2.

Fill the can with water and freeze until firm.

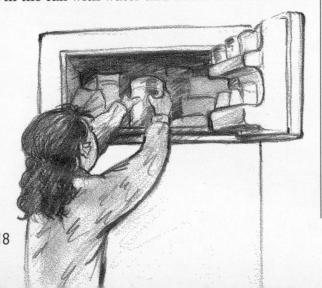

3.

Run warm water on the side of the can to loosen the ice, turn the can upside down in a sink and gently shake the ice out.

4.

Remove the Plasticine and return the ice cylinder to the freezer.

5.

To use, place a tea-candle in the hollow left by the Plasticine. Don't forget to put a saucer underneath when you light it. Blow out the candle and return the candleholder to the freezer before you leave the room.

OUTDOOR CANDLES

Create a winter wonderland with twinkling candles buried in a snowbank or tucked behind a pyramid of snowballs. Remember to blow out the candles before you leave.

- Push a gloved fist 15 cm (6 in.) into a deep bank of shoveled snow. Wedge in a candle stub, making sure the candle is out of the wind. With an adult's help, carefully light the candle with a long-handled match and watch the snowbank glow.

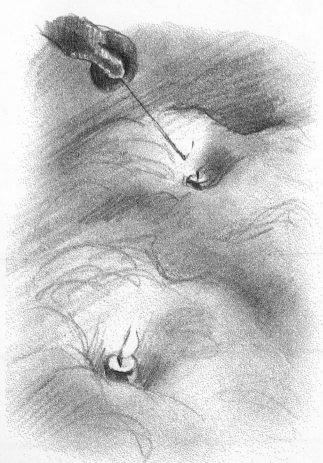

- Wedge a candle into the snow. Make 25 firm snowballs the size of grapefruits. Form a circular base around the candle, using 9 snowballs. Each ball just touches the next. Make a snow pyramid with 7 balls in the next circle, then 5 and 3. Save 1 snowball for the top. Carefully light the candle with a long-handled match through a hole in the side of the pyramid. When you want to snuff out the candle, place the last snowball on the top. When it melts, it will drip down on the candle.

WARM-ME-UP SOUP

When you just can't shake the shivers, you need a bowl of warm homemade soup. First, make this tasty, golden broth. Always wear oven mitts and have an adult help with the stove.

THE BROTH

You'll need:
the bones left over from a chicken or turkey dinner or 4 stock cubes
2 L (2 quarts) cold water
4 peppercorns
1 bay leaf
3 sprigs of parsley
1 onion
1 stalk celery
1 carrot
2 large pots, a strainer, a spoon

1.
Put all the ingredients in a pot and simmer on low for 3 hours or until the water is reduced by half. Turn off the stove and let the pot cool down.

2.
When cool, strain just the broth into the other pot. Throw out the bones and boiled vegetables.

3.
Chill the broth in the refrigerator.

4.
With a spoon, scrape off and discard the fat that hardens on the top of the chilled stock. The cold chicken broth underneath will be like jelly. Now you are ready to make the soup on the next page.

THE SOUP

Use your broth to make a soup guaranteed to beat the cold.

You'll need:
15 mL (1 tablespoon) butter, margarine or vegetable oil
1 chopped stalk of celery
1 chopped onion
750 mL (3 cups) cold broth
400 mL (1½ cups) chopped raw vegetables such as carrots, peeled potatoes, mushrooms, broccoli stems, cabbage and turnips
a frying pan, a pot

1.
Melt the butter in the frying pan and add the celery and onion. Cook on medium-low until the pieces soften.

2.
Add the cooked celery and onion to a pot containing the broth and the chopped raw vegetables.

3.
Bring to a boil and then simmer on the stove for about 30 minutes or until all the vegetables are tender. Stir occasionally.

4.
Serve in bowls or mugs. Add salt and pepper to taste. Store leftovers in the fridge.

THE EXTRAS

When you're extra hungry or need a boost of energy, add cooked pasta spirals, shells or macaroni to your homemade soup.

21

FLEECE FUN

With these fleece mitts and headband you'll be cozy all winter long. Look for bright-colored or printed fleece.

MITTS

You'll need:

paper, a pencil, a ruler and scissors
fleece
straight pins
a needle and thread
decorative buttons (optional)

1.
To make a pattern, lay one hand on the paper. Trace around the outside of the hand, stopping at the wrist.

2.
For a cuff, add 10 cm (4 in.) below the wrist. Make this wider than the wrist so that the hand will fit into the finished mitt.

3.
Draw another 2 cm (³/₄ in.) line around the outside of the hand outline. Cut it out along this line.

4.
Fold the fleece in half, good sides together (if there is a good or patterned side). Pin the paper pattern to the fleece and cut around it.

5.
Remove the pattern and pin the two fleece pieces together.

6.
Thread a needle and knot the thread. Use small stitches to sew around the outside of the mitt. Repeat steps 4 to 6 to make another mitt.

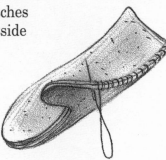

7.
Turn the cuffs over about 4 cm (1¹/₂ in.) and decorate by sewing on buttons or cutouts in a contrasting color of fleece. If you choose to leave the mitts plain, they will be reversible.

HEADBAND

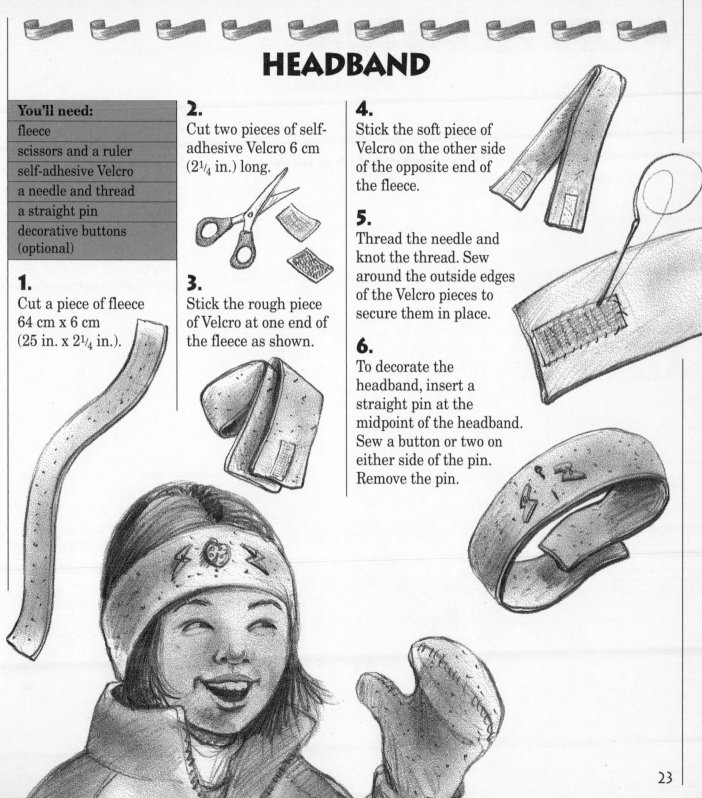

You'll need:

fleece

scissors and a ruler

self-adhesive Velcro

a needle and thread

a straight pin

decorative buttons (optional)

1.
Cut a piece of fleece 64 cm x 6 cm (25 in. x 2¼ in.).

2.
Cut two pieces of self-adhesive Velcro 6 cm (2¼ in.) long.

3.
Stick the rough piece of Velcro at one end of the fleece as shown.

4.
Stick the soft piece of Velcro on the other side of the opposite end of the fleece.

5.
Thread the needle and knot the thread. Sew around the outside edges of the Velcro pieces to secure them in place.

6.
To decorate the headband, insert a straight pin at the midpoint of the headband. Sew a button or two on either side of the pin. Remove the pin.

23

MORE FLEECE FUN

Keep your neck toasty-warm with a fleece bandana or scarf.

BANDANA

You'll need:

1 sheet of newspaper
a measuring tape, a pencil and scissors
fleece
straight pins
5 cm (2 in.) self-adhesive Velcro
a needle and thread

1.
To make a pattern, draw a triangle on the newspaper with the following measurements.

50 cm (20 in.)

35 cm (14 in.)

2.
Cut out along the lines, rounding the corners if you wish.

3.
Pin the pattern on a piece of fleece and cut out the triangle. Remove the pins.

4.
Stick the rough piece of Velcro at one end of the neckwarmer as shown.

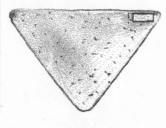

5.
Stick the soft piece of Velcro to the other side at the opposite end of the neckwarmer.

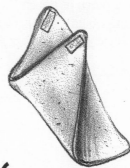

6.
Thread the needle and knot the thread. Sew around the outside edges of the Velcro to hold them in place.

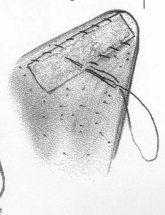

SCARF

You'll need:

a measuring tape or stick

a piece of chalk

scissors

fleece

a darning needle and
embroidery thread
(optional)

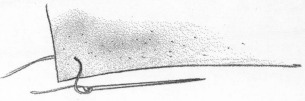

1.

Use the chalk to mark
a 20 cm x 130 cm
(8 in. x 50 in.)
piece of fleece.
Cut it out.

2.

Finish the edges, using a blanket stitch all around
or blanket stitch just the long sides and cut
fringes at each end.

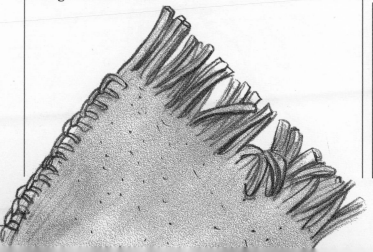

BLANKET STITCH

You'll need:

a darning needle and embroidery thread of the same
or contrasting color to your fleece

1.

Thread the needle and make a knot. Pull the
needle and thread through the edge of the fabric.

2.

Bring the needle under the edge of the fleece,
then poke it back up through with the needle
pointing toward the outside edge. Pull the needle
through the loop. Pull gently to tighten.

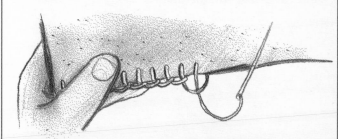

COZY LAP BLANKET

When you're good at blanket stitching, try
trimming the edges of a blanket-sized piece
of fleece to snuggle under.

KNITTING A SCARF

The air outdoors may be freezing cold, but the air pockets in knitted wool will keep you warmer than any other fabric.

There is no right or wrong way to knit. Most people hold the work with the left hand and knit with the right hand. If you're left-handed you can knit this way or reverse these directions.

You'll need:
Shetland Ragg craft wool
1 pair 6.0 mm (size 10) needles
a measuring tape

1.

Cast on: Make a slip knot 15 cm (6 in.) from the end of the wool. Slip it onto one needle and pull until the stitch is loose enough to move easily on the needle. The stitch should be 2.5 cm (1 in.) from the tip of the needle.

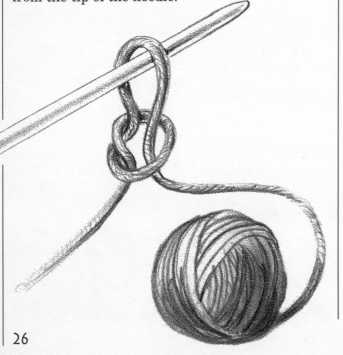

2.

Hold this needle in your left hand with the pointer finger on top of the stitch, the thumb to the left of the stitch, and the remaining three fingers supporting the needle from below.

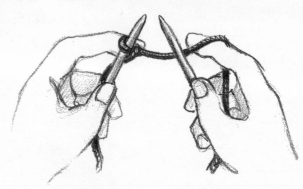

3.

Slide the right needle up through the stitch. Pick up the wool in your right hand and wrap it around the right needle, pulling it snuggly between the needles.

4.

Pull the wool to the right using the right pointer finger and support the needle with the thumb on the top and the remaining fingers below the needle. Use the left pointer finger to push the right needle under the left needle toward your left thumb.

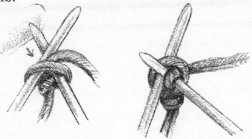

5.

A new stitch will now be on the tip of the right needle. Slide this stitch onto the left needle being careful not to drop the previously made stitch. Repeat until there are 30 stitches cast on.

6.

Knitting: Repeat steps three and four, completing the stitch by pulling the right and left needles apart, causing the new stitch to move onto the right needle. Knit until all 30 stitches are on the right needle. Switch the needles to the opposite hands and begin again. Repeat until the scarf measures 1 m (3 ft.). At the beginning of the next row, cast off.

7.

Cast off: Knit two stitches. Slip the left needle through the left side of the right-hand stitch. Lift the stitch up and over the top of the second stitch, leaving only the second stitch on the right-hand needle.

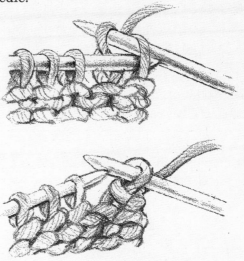

8.

Knit another stitch and repeat step 7 until the last stitch remains. Cut the wool 20 cm (8 in.) from the stitch. Holding the knitting with the left hand, pull the needle until the stitch becomes a big loop, and the remaining wool slips through it.

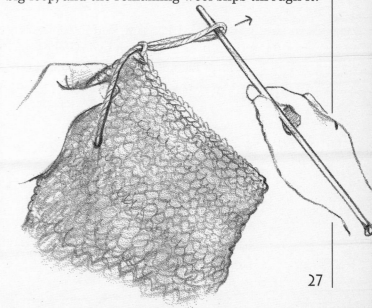

KNITTING A HAT

Once you've knit the scarf or page 26, you're ready to make this wooly hat.

You'll need:
chunky craft wool such as Shetland Ragg
1 pair 6.0 mm (size 10) needles
a measuring tape
scissors
a darning needle

1.
Cast on 64 stitches (see page 26, steps 1 to 5). Knit for 20 cm (8 in.).

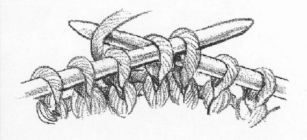

2.
At the beginning of the next row, knit 2 together by passing the right needle through two stitches and knitting as before. Then knit 6, knit 2 together, knit 6, knit 2 together across the row.

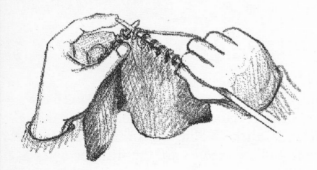

3.
Knit 1 row. Then knit another row in which you knit 5, knit 2 together, knit 5, knit 2 together, across the entire row.

4.
Knit 1 row. Then knit 4, knit 2 together, knit 4 and so on until 16 stitches remain. Knit 2 together 8 times.

5.
Cut the wool 60 cm (24 in.) from the work. Thread the end with a darning needle. Using the darning needle as a knitting needle, slip the remaining 8 stitches onto the wool end.

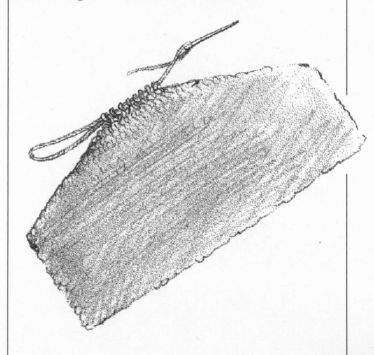

6.

Pull until the stitches form a circle at the top of the hat.

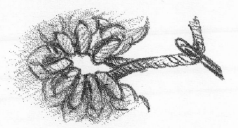

7.

Fold the hat in half. Pinch the edges together and sew with the whip stitch as shown until 5 cm (2 in.) from the open end of the hat.

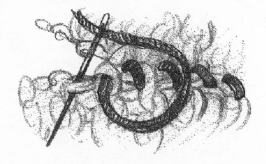

8.

Turn the edges to the inside and continue sewing to the lower edge.

9.

Finish off by stitching back through the work for 5 cm (2 in.). Carefully use scissors to trim the remaining wool from the needle. Turn the hat right side out and roll up the brim 5 cm (2 in.).

COOL EXPERIMENT

Try this cool experiment. Are you warmer wearing a hat and no mitts OR mitts and no hat? What can you conclude from your observations?

Answer: Body heat escapes the fastest through the head.

SNOW SCIENCE

What is freezing cold but makes a warm blanket? What grows on dirt but is sparkling clean? Snow, of course! Fill a measuring cup with a handful of fresh snow. Let the snow melt and take a look.

- You'll see there's much less water in the cup than there was snow. That's because snow is filled with tiny air pockets. When the snow melts, the air escapes. The air pockets in snow act as insulation so that animals and people can live in snow houses and keep warm.

- At the bottom of the cup, you'll see specks of dirt. That's because snowflakes form when snow crystals collect on airborne dust and dirt particles. The crystals actually grow on the dirt. When snow melts, the dirt is left behind.

SNOWFLAKE IMPRESSIONS

See just how intricate newly fallen snowflakes can be.

You'll need:
hairspray (CFC-free)
a small pane of glass
a magnifying glass

1.

Spray one side of the pane of glass with hairspray and place it in the freezer.

2.

When it snows, carefully carry the pane outside with the hairspray side up and let a few snowflakes fall on it. Look at them with the magnifying glass.

3.

Carefully take the pane inside and let the snowflakes melt. Use your magnifying glass to look at the impressions left on the pane.

FLAKE SHAPES

No one has ever found two snowflakes that are exactly the same — but most are six sided. Each snowflake is made up of snow crystals — very large flakes may contain up to 200 crystals. Look for these snowflake shapes in fresh snow:

- hexagonal prisms

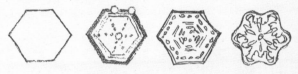

- stellar crystals

- hexagonal columns

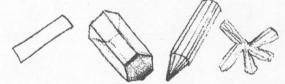

- needles

- spatial dendrites

31

DRAFT BUSTER

Wind is whistling in the window. Warm air is being sucked outside from under the door. Shiverrrr! It's not a ghost; it's air currents at work. Outwit these natural drafts with a draft-busting snake wedged at the bottom of the door.

You'll need:
2 colors of fleece or felt
a measuring tape, a ruler, chalk, scissors, straight pins
a needle and embroidery thread
wool (or cotton) stuffing
a long-handled wooden spoon

1.

For the body, measure and cut two fleece or felt pieces 1 m x 15 cm (3 ft. x 6 in.).

2.

To shape the tail, use the chalk or a light-colored pencil to draw a 30 cm (12 in.) "V" at one end.

32

3.

To shape the head, find the midpoint and mark 2 cm (³/₄ in.) on either side. From each of these points, draw an 8 cm (3 in.) line to the edge of the fabric.

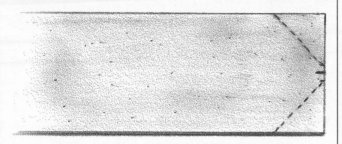

4.

Pin the two pieces together. Using the blanket stitch (see page 25), sew around the outside of the snake, leaving the head end open.

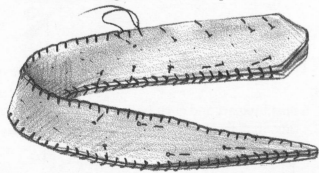

5.

Use the spoon handle to push stuffing into the tail. Do not overstuff.

6.

With a contrasting color of fleece or felt, cut out two eyes the size of bottle caps. Stitch the eyes on the head of one side of the snake. Cut out a forked tongue 3 cm x 6 cm (1¹/₈ in. x 2¹/₄ in.).

7.

Fill the head with stuffing and place the tongue so that it sticks out the end of the snake. Pin the two pieces of fabric together and blanket stitch around the sides of the head.

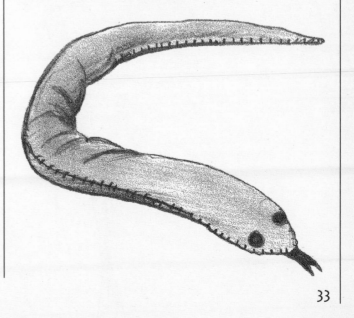

33

WARM BY THE FIRE

There's nothing like a crackling fire to warm up a snowy day. If you have a fireplace, make this log carrier to help collect wood.

You'll need:
2.5 m (8 ft.) narrow bias tape (cloth)
a 90 cm x 60 cm (3 ft. x 2 ft.) piece of canvas
scissors
straight pins
a strong needle and polyester thread
2 dowels or smooth peeled sticks, about 60 cm (2 ft.) long and 2 cm ($^3/_4$ in.) thick

1.

Pin bias tape down both long sides of the canvas. Sew with short stitches near the inside edge of the tape through the tape and the canvas.

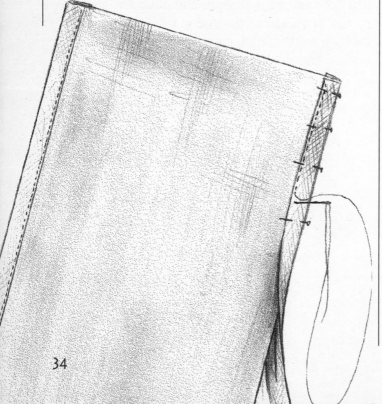

2.

Cut a half circle out of the middle of both ends of the canvas. The half circle should begin 20 cm (8 in.) in from either end of the canvas and end no more than 10 cm (4 in.) into the canvas.

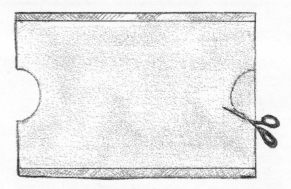

3.

Pin bias tape around each half circle end and sew the tape in place.

4.

Make a tube on the ends of the canvas by folding the canvas over 6 cm ($2^1/_4$ in.). Pin and sew in place on both sides of the half circles.

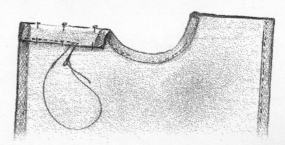

5.

Slide the dowels or sticks through the tubes. The half circle openings will make handles to grip at each side.

6.

Lay the canvas flat. Pile several logs in the middle. Pick up the two dowels or sticks to carry the logs.

TIPS FOR STARTING A FIREPLACE FIRE

1.

Ask an adult to help you check that the damper is open.

2.

Bunch up several handfuls of paper and place them in the center back of the fireplace.

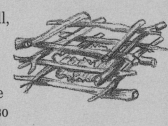

3.

Place about 12 small, dry twigs (kindling wood) around the paper in a log cabin shape, leaving space between each twig so the fire can breathe.

4.

Stand 4 or 5 larger sticks in a teepee shape over the kindling, leaving air spaces.

5.

Light the paper. Close the fireplace screen or doors when the kindling catches fire. **Never leave the fire unattended.**

FIRESIDE STORIES

A cold and stormy night is a great start to a story. Gather family and friends around the fire and tell a chilling story, or start everyone giggling with a crazy word game.

A B C D E F G H I J K L M N O P Q R S T U V W X Y Z

WINTER ALPHABET STORIES

Sit in a circle and decide who will be the first storyteller. The story starts with "It was a cold and stormy night when . . ." The first person adds a few sentences to the story and ends with a winter word beginning with the letter "a," such as antifreeze. The next person picks up the thread of the story, adds to it and ends with a word beginning with "b," such as blizzard. Continue through the alphabet, helping each other out with the hard letters. How many winter words start with "X"? That's an x-tremely hard question.

numb · mittens · drift · icicle · cold · arctic · reindeer · snowy owl · jacket · frozen · windchill · sleet · blubber · quilt · hockey

SILLY STORY GAME

All you need is paper, pencils, erasers and imagination for this wild word game.

1.

Each person writes a simple short story featuring local landmarks, family and friends. The story can be real or made up. Set a time limit of 10 or 15 minutes for story writing.

2.

Using an eraser, remove several nouns (persons, places or things) and a verb (action word) in each sentence, leaving blank spaces in their places.

3.

Sit as a group and, without reading the story aloud, the first person asks the group for winter words to fill in the blanks in her story — such as "a noun," "a verb," "another noun." When all the blanks are filled, she reads the story to everyone.

Every morning Grandma ___VERB___ out the ___NOUN___ and watches the clouds, ___NOUN___ and waves on the ___NOUN___. Then she ___VERB___ us which way the ___NOUN___ is blowing. This helps ___NOUN___ decide what she will ___VERB___ that day. If the ___NOUN___ blows from the east, the ___NOUN___ will be cold and she won't ___VERB___. Instead she might ___VERB___ or go sailing.

STORY STICK

There is a tradition at the council meeting of Native Americans — whoever is holding the stick has the right to speak. If everyone in your family talks at once, command their attention with a piece of driftwood or an unusual stick. Talk when you're holding the stick and listen when you're not. Once you've had your say, pass the stick to the next person.

OUTDOOR WINTER FUN

Short winter days can still be packed full of outdoor fun. Learn what's swimming under the ice while you're playing a game of hog on top of it. Find out about life — and death — under the snow. Make your own snowshoes and follow the tracks of the creatures that venture out in the cold. Or, map out a winter trail complete with trail markers and cairns. Then test your skills at cross-country skiing. When the games and exploring have exhausted you, enjoy a winter picnic.

SNOW FORTS

When the snow is sticky enough to pack a snowball and there's plenty of it, the conditions are good for building a snow fort. Choose a site where you can see in all directions and spy any unwanted intruders. Your spot should be shaded some of the time so the fort will not melt away on a sunny day.

SNOW FORT

1.

Roll a large snowball around, so it picks up snow until it's as big and heavy as you can make it. Roll it to your fort site, pat the sides square and place it as the first block in your fort wall.

2.

Roll another snowball until it's the same size as the first snowball. Push it in place beside the first block.

3.

Continue until you have a ring of snowball blocks outlining your fort. Leave an opening for a back door.

4.

On the outside, pack snow into the spaces between the blocks. Place smaller snowball blocks on top of the base ring. If you have left-over boughs from holiday decorations, stick them into the top of the snow blocks to add height and privacy.

5.

Smooth the inside walls of your fort. Pack and carve the snow to make benches and shelves, if you like.

SNOW CITADEL

When the snow is deep and dry, you can make a fortress city, or citadel, with the help of a shovel. Look for a grove of small trees such as sumac or aspen. **Do not tunnel into the snow because a snow roof may collapse.** Instead, shovel out snow paths between the trunks to make passageways and then widen some to make rooms. Sumac trunks are usually spaced apart while the branches interweave overhead. Those branches, heavy with red tassels of fruit, will form an open-air roof to your citadel as well as a feeding area for local birds and squirrels.

Another good place to make a citadel is in a stand of young evergreen trees. After a snowfall, you'll find that little snow collects close to the trunks of bushy evergreens. Look for trees that have lower branches high enough from the ground that you can sit or stand under them beside the trunks. Shake any snow off the boughs above and clear out the area below with a shovel to make rooms. Finally, shovel trails to connect your snow rooms. The tree boughs will make a natural roof over each room.

FUN IN THE SNOW

Snow is the main ingredient in all these outdoor games and activities.

SNOW SOCCER

Set the boundaries of the soccer pitch. A rectangular space is ideal but not necessary. Declare trees, rocks, buildings and hazards out of bounds. Set up a goal about 2 m (6½ ft.) wide at either end of the soccer pitch. Players should wear treaded winter boots and layers of clothing, including a hat, gloves and warm pants.

1.

Divide into two teams of three or four players each. Teams choose one defense player and the rest are forwards. It's too cold for a goalie.

2.

The ball is placed in the center of the pitch. With the ball between them, one player from each team faces each other. At the count of three, they try to gain possession of the ball using feet, knees and heads, but no hands.

3.

Players try to kick the ball into the goal of the opposite team. Each goal counts for one point.

4.

When one team hits the ball out of bounds, a member of the other team throws the ball back into play.

5.

When the teams are worn out and ready for a cup of hot chocolate, one player calls, "last goal wins!"

TARGET PRACTICE

Using a snowball, pack a snow bull's eye ring on the side of a tree or a brick wall with no windows. The snow will catch in the rough surface and be easy to see. Take turns aiming for the target. Who can hit the target most often?

Throwing snowballs is irresistible, but never throw them at people, pets or vehicles. Stick to target practice!

SAY IT WITH SNOW

Spell out a short and simple message, such as Happy Birthday, Dad or Happy Holidays using a water bottle filled with water and food coloring. If the temperature is below freezing, the message will be visible until the next snowfall.

HOPSCOTCH IN THE SNOW

Use a water bottle filled with water and food coloring to outline a hopscotch board on the snow. Throw a snowball into the first square, hop over it, then hop into every square up to number 10.

On the way back, stop to pick up your snowball. Now toss the snowball into number 2. You're out if you step on the colored lines or in a square containing another player's snowball.

ICE AND SNOW ART

If you like making sandcastles in the summer, you'll love ice sculpting. Plan this activity for when the weather is below freezing.

ICE CASTLES

1.

With an adult's permission, collect as many containers as possible, including: loaf, cake and muffin tins; yogurt, ice cream and margarine tubs; large and small pails; ice-cube trays and plastic cups. Spread the containers on a flat area, outdoors.

2.

Use a watering can to fill the containers. Allow to freeze overnight or until solid.

3.

Remove the ice shapes from their molds by squeezing the outside of the containers, inverting and tapping the bottom. Use a little snow to glue the shapes together. Letting your imagination guide you, decide what to make. It could be something wild and crazy or a standard castle.

4.

For a glistening finish, sprinkle lightly with water. You can color the water with drink crystals or food coloring.

MAKE YOUR OWN SCULPTING SNOW

If nature won't cooperate, it is possible to manufacture a block of sculpting snow.

You'll need
a shovel
a watering can
a garden trowel
waterproof boots

1.

Make a small mound of snow, sprinkle with water and pat with the back of the shovel. Add more snow and repeat this process until you have a large block of icy snow.

2.

Using a garden trowel, scoop or carve away some snow, leaving behind the desired shape. You can transform the snow into works of art. Feature the creatures whose fur or feathers change color in winter to adapt to their surroundings — the arctic fox, the snowshoe hare or the white-tailed rabbit, least weasel, snowy owl and ptarmigan. Sprinkle the final product with water.

SNOW ANGELS

Made any snow angels lately? Why not try a chain of angels? You can do this by yourself or with a bunch of friends.

TRADITIONAL SNOW GAMES

The first people of North America played games that combined fun with hunting practice. Play these Native outdoor winter games and increase your ability to throw with power, speed and accuracy.

SNOW SNAKE

The object of snow snake is to throw bone darts to see whose travels farthest along an ice run.

You'll need:

fine sandpaper
a clean pork or beef rib bone or a smooth 15 cm (6 in.) stick
a hand drill with a fine bit
2 feathers or evergreen pieces, each about 4 times as long as the bone
white glue
a shovel

1.
With the sandpaper, smooth the sides of the bone.

2.
Ask an adult to drill a hole in one end of the bone.

3.
Put glue on the shaft end of the feathers (or evergreen) and insert into the hole at the end of the bone.

4.
Shovel a straight stretch of ice or pack down and water a long trench of snow to make a narrow ice run.

5.
Throw the bone dart overhand or sidearm along the run. Draw lines or sprinkle colored drink crystals in the snow to show where each player's dart stops.

6.
For variation, construct a snow ramp along the run so the darts "take off" partway along. Old stories claim that, in ancient times, snow-snake darts launched from ramps could fly up to a kilometer (about half a mile).

NARWHAL STRIKE

For some time, scientists puzzled over the purpose of circular stone rings on the arctic tundra. Each ring is about 1 m (3 ft.) across and is placed inside a slightly longer, oval ring. Following a discussion with Native elders, scientists concluded that these rings represent kayaks and form the play area of an ancient game for two players. One player walked around the outer oval ring dragging a strip of animal hide or rope. The other player would sit in the inner ring with a stick and, without moving from the circle, try to strike the rope on the ground as it passed. This is the kind of move a skilled hunter would make, sitting in his kayak, trying to spear a seal or a narwhal in the sea.

You can try this game with a friend using a ring of snowballs to outline the round kayak seat and a larger oval ring of snowballs to show the outline of the kayak itself. One player drags a rope while the seated player tries to touch the moving rope with a blunt stick, such as a hockey stick.

47

MAKE A RINK

Construct your own ice rink for skating, sliding and game playing — until the spring thaw.

1.

With an adult's help, decide where to locate the rink. Remove all hazards such as rocks. Pile snow, straw or used tires around trees and other immovable objects.

2.

Shovel snow onto the rink area and stamp it down with your boots. When the weather forecast predicts temperatures will stay below freezing for several days, soak the prepared rink area using a garden hose or a sprinkler. Repeat for several days in a row until the ice is at least 2 cm (3/4 in.) thick. Do not walk on the rink while it's under construction.

3.

Once the rink is ready, keep it shoveled and use a hose to flood any cracks that appear now or later when the ice chips.

4.

If you use the rink at night, consider building a winter fire beside it (see page 112).

Note: Hoses and outdoor taps can freeze and burst in cold weather. After flooding the rink, turn off the tap and drain the hose completely. Ask an adult if there is an indoor turn-off valve that should be opened and closed with each use.

SKATING THREESOME

With two friends, test the new rink with this game.

- Three skaters hold hands and begin skating together in one line. The middle skater plants his skates by digging in the inside edges and swings the two outside skaters forward.

- When they are at arm's length, they plant their skates and pull the middle skater up and past them to arm's length.

- He plants his skates and swings the outside skaters forward again. Keep going as long as possible.

ICE SAFETY

Skating on ponds, lakes and rivers is a fun part of winter, but if someone falls through the ice, there are only minutes to react. Always ask an adult to make sure the ice is safe. If you're not sure, don't go onto the ice.

RINK GAMES

The games begin as soon as the ice is ready (see page 48). Strap on the blades, drop the puck and start with a game of shinny.

SHINNY

1.
Set up a 2 m (6½ ft.) wide goal at each end of the rink. Use snow boots or milk jugs filled with water as goal posts.

2.
Each player needs skates or warm boots with good treads and a hockey stick. Divide into two evenly skilled teams of three to eight players each.

3.
Teams choose a goalie and one or two players to play defense. The rest are forwards.

4.
Place the puck or ball on the ice in the center of the rink. The game begins with a face-off between one player from each team. These two players say together, "one, two, three, game on" and try to gain possession of the puck.

5.
Players try to shoot the puck past the goalie of the opposite team. Each goal counts as one point.

50

HOG

When there are not enough players to divide into shinny teams, try a game of hog. The object of the game is to prevent the others from scoring while scoring the most points yourself. Whoever hogs the puck the most usually wins.

KEEP-AWAY

Played with two players, you try to keep the puck away from your opponent as long as possible. This requires skillful stick-handling and fancy skating.

RINK BOWLING

1.
Fill the bottom of 10 large pop bottles with about 5 cm (2 in.) of sand or gravel. Tighten the lids.

2.
For bowling balls, you'll need 2 empty soup or coffee cans for each player. Fill them with water and set outside to freeze.

3.
The bowling "alley" can be up to 18 m (60 ft.) long. Mark a start line at one end of the rink using drink crystals.

4.
Set up a triangle of 10 bowling pin bottles at the other end.

5.
For each turn, players take 2 throws. Clear away fallen bottles between throws. The player with the most points after 10 turns is the winner.

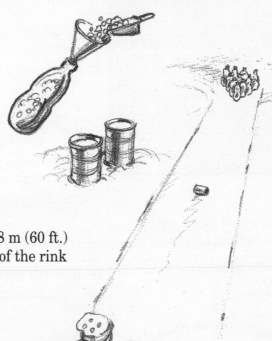

KEEPING SCORE

- 1 point is scored for each bottle knocked down

- 10 bottles knocked down with the first ball (a strike) = 10 points

- Reset the bottles, throw the second ball and score 1 point for each additional bottle knocked down up to 10 points — 20 points in total

- Some bottles knocked down with the first ball and the remainder with the second ball (a spare) = 10 points in total

51

SNOWSHOES

With a pair of snowshoes to spread your weight over the snow — and a little practice — you can easily walk across deep drifts. You'll require an extra set of hands for this project, so ask an adult to help you.

You'll need:

2 lengths of peeled, green shrub willow, or aspen, about 2 m (6½ ft.) long and 2.5 cm (1 in.) thick for each snowshoe

a hammer

spiral nails (like screws, available at hardware stores)

2 10 cm (4 in.) lengths of thin wire

pliers

pruning clippers

a hand drill with a fine bit and a 7 mm (¼ in.) bit

10 m (32 ft.) of nylon cord for each snowshoe

4 strong mesh orange bags or onion bags

1.

With your thumbs, carefully work one willow length into a loop frame so the ends cross. Hammer a spiral nail through the crossed ends. Reinforce the join by wrapping wire around it. Twist the wire tight with pliers.

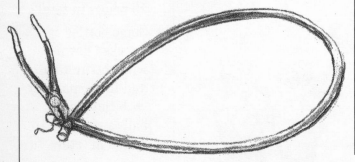

2.

Lay the frame on the ground and put your boot in the middle. With the pruning shears, cut two bars that are the width of the frame from the second piece of willow. One bar should fit across the frame above the toe and one behind the heel of your boot.

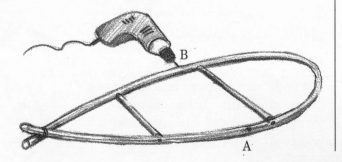

3.

With the two bars in place, drill a nail hole from the outside of the frame into both ends of each bar. Hammer spiral nails into the drill holes.

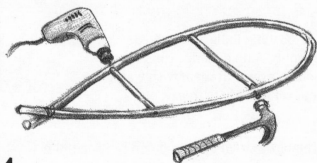

4.

Drill a hole into each side of the frame 4 cm (1½ in.) below the toe bar. Label the holes *A* and *B*.

5.
Pull the nylon cord through *A*, knot it, then pull across through *B* and back through *A*. This is *A-B*.

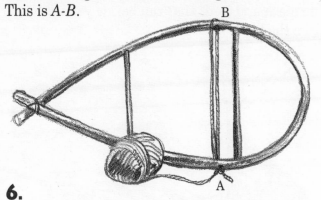

6.
Pull the free end of the cord tightly over the toe bar, down to the heel bar, up to the toe bar and back to the heel bar, working across the snowshoe from *A*.

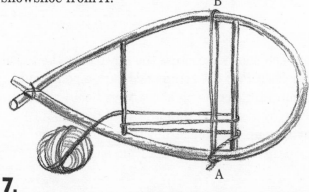

7.
Wrap two loops of the cord from the heel bar up to *A-B* and back (this will make a toe space). Then wrap two loops from the heel to toe bar, ending at *B*.

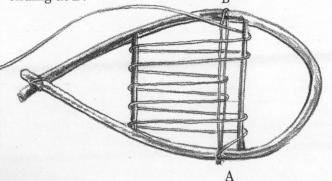

8.
Now weave the cord over and under back along *A-B*. Reinforce with extra loops around the toe space and knot the cord, but do not cut it.

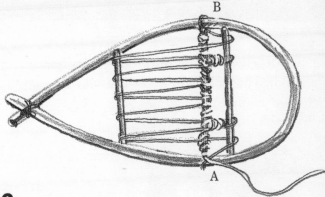

9.
Cut the bottoms off two mesh bags so they slip over the frame, one from the toe to the toe bar and the other from the heel to the heel bar. Lash the mesh to the frame and bars by threading the nylon cord through holes in the mesh and then winding it around the frame, over and over, pulling and knotting until the mesh is attached tightly.

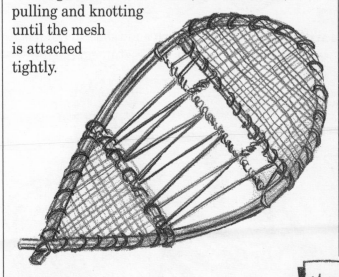

10.
Repeat steps 1 to 9 for the second snowshoe.

MORE

LACING YOUR SNOWSHOES

You'll need:

a pair of warm boots with a soft, rounded heel

2 2 m (6½ ft.) nylon straps, belts or cotton lamp wick

1.

Lay the snowshoes on the ground. If either snowshoe has a bow in it, lay the snowshoe so the toe points up.

2.

With boots on, step on each snowshoe so the toe is just below the toe bar and resting on the toe space.

3.

Place the middle of the straps over the toes of your boots. Weave each end down and up through the mesh and cords that run beside your boots from the toe to heel bars.

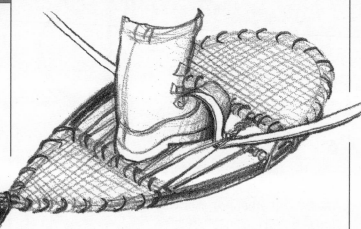

4.

For each snowshoe, cross the strap over the top of your boot. Pull the strap ends back on each side of your ankle crossing above your heel. Pull them to the front of your shin and then back to tie partway up your leg. Adjust so your heel can move up and down but not from side to side.

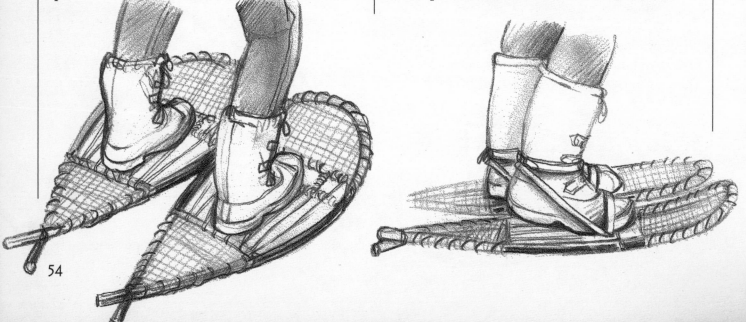

WALKING IN YOUR SNOWSHOES

Because you have woven cord into the center section of each snowshoe, they will have a little bounce to help you walk. Your heel should lift with each step and your toe should press into the toe space. At first it will feel funny to walk with your feet so far apart, but with practice you may even be able to run.

BIG FOOT

The ancient people who invented snowshoes probably took the idea from wild animals. Polar bears, snowshoe hares, lynx and others that survive by running in deep snow have extra-large feet for their size. With big feet, their body weight is spread over a greater area, and they are more likely to stay on top of the snow without sinking.

CROSS-COUNTRY SKIING

Northerners have cross-country skied for thousands of years. A 4500-year-old rock carving on Rodoy Island, Norway, shows a skier gliding smoothly downhill. It's a great winter sport. Here are some tips to get you started:

- You'll have control and fun if you wear skis that come up to your wrists when your arms are stretched overhead. But, when you gain control, you'll find that longer skis give a better glide. Poles should come no higher than your shoulder.

- Dress in layers for cross-country skiing. Pull on a hat and a small backpack. When you work up a sweat, you can take layers off and store them in your pack. Then, when you feel cold — or when you stop for a rest — put them back on again.

- Many skis have prepared undersides that need no wax for smooth downhill gliding or easy uphill climbing. However, it's a good idea to carry a block of clear paraffin wax in case you ski over a patch of melted snow. When slush packs onto your ski bottoms, take off your skis, scrape away the sticky snow or ice and rub the bottom with a coat of wax. Try to rub one way, tip to heel, for a better slide.

SKIING ON A STRAIGHTAWAY

Cross-country skiing is like exaggerated walking — big arm movements with long sliding steps.

1.

Plant your left ski pole in the snow on the outside of your left ski and slide your right ski forward.

2.

While pulling your left ski pole out of the snow, plant your right pole in and slide your left ski forward.

3.

Keep working until you build up momentum and are sliding smoothly.

MORE

DOWNHILL

On an easy slope with no rocks, trees or hazards, learn to snowplow. Point your tips slightly toward each other while you push down hard on the inside edges with your ski boots. The more you point the ski tips toward each other and the harder you press on the inside edges of your ski boots, the slower your slide will be. Practice until you can snowplow to a stop.

When you want to go a little faster, move your feet until your skis no longer point toward each other but are parallel. Bend your knees slightly and lean forward. Tuck your poles against your sides and let yourself slide. When you want to slow down, return to the snowplow.

To turn left, put your weight on your left ski and twist your right hip, shoulder and ski into the turn. To turn right, put your weight on your right ski and steer your left hip, shoulder and ski into the turn.

CLIMBING UPHILL

Lean forward, dig in your poles and walk up a small hill. If you start to slide backward, try walking with your tips pointing out and your heels pointing in to make a large herringbone pattern in the snow. If the grade is so steep that you still slide back, turn and sidestep up the hill.

WINTER TRAIL

Clear a trail for cross-country skiing, snowshoeing or hiking.

- Plan the path of your trail in early winter before much snow covers the ground. Then you can follow the natural lines and openings of the land and avoid objects hidden by snow.

- Mark the route with streamers of bright ribbon or fluorescent tape tied to shrubs and trees at eye level. Markers should be placed so you can see one behind you and one ahead wherever you stand on the trail. Over time, your trail may mark the landscape itself in which case you will be able to cut down the markers.

- In places where there are few trees or shrubs, make tall rock piles, or cairns, that will jut above snow level to mark the pathway. Where the trail turns direction, place a pointer rock on the top of a cairn to show the new direction.

- Wearing work gloves, clear the path of fallen leaves, sticks and movable rocks. You might need a garden rake or shovel for this job.

- In most places, your trail need only be as wide as one person. To make it safer for skiers, widen the trail where it skirts rocks, comes near low branches or makes sharp turns.

- Make a map of your trail marking important landmarks, good views, wildlife sightings, cairns and other information.

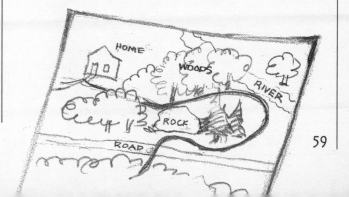

WINTER PICNIC

A winter picnic outside can be sandwiched between skiing, skating, fort building or any activity that keeps you warm. If you pull these snacks from your backpack, you'll be refueled for more fun.

CHICKEN NOODLE-DOG SOUP

You'll need:

a non-breakable Thermos with a cup lid

chicken noodle soup

a chicken hot dog

a fork

1.

Fill the Thermos with hot tap water to warm it up inside.

2.

Heat a can or packet of chicken noodle soup according to the directions on the package.

3.

Pour the water out of the Thermos. Place the chicken dog into the Thermos and fill with chicken noodle soup.

4.

Screw on the Thermos cap and put the Thermos and fork in your backpack. When lunchtime comes, drink the soup and then eat the chicken dog, holding it with the fork.

TRAIL BARS

You'll need:

75 mL (⅓ cup) margarine

175 mL (¾ cup) honey

125 mL (½ cup) brown sugar

500 mL (2 cup) rolled oats

250 mL (1 cup) bran

250 mL (1 cup) shelled sunflower seeds

250 mL (1 cup) chopped dried fruit, such as raisins, apricots, etc.

125 mL (½ cup) chopped nuts, such as walnuts (or extra dried fruit)

50 mL (¼ cup) sesame seeds

a small pot, a small bowl, a large bowl, a baking dish and plastic or foil wrap

1.
In the pot, melt the margarine over low heat on the stove.

2.
Add honey and sugar and bring to a boil. Turn down the heat and simmer for 5 minutes.

3.
Remove from heat to cool. While it cools, in a large bowl combine the rest of the ingredients.

4.
Stir the honey, sugar and margarine mixture into the mixed dry ingredients.

5.
Press the mixture into the baking dish and bake at 180°C (350°F) for 15 minutes.

6.
Let cool and then cut into squares.

7.
Wrap individual squares in plastic or foil wrap and put them in your backpack.

EASY ENERGIZER BISCUITS

If you don't have time to bake ahead, make a pile of soda cracker sandwiches with cheese or peanut butter spread between the crackers. Wrap in plastic and pack carefully so the crackers won't break.

MAKING TRACKS

When the ground is covered with snow, food is scarce and many creatures are hibernating. Animal sightings are rare. But there are often signs of nocturnal or secretive visitors. Learn to identify snow prints. Can you tell if the animal was sauntering along, running or being chased? Then check some trees for animal signs.

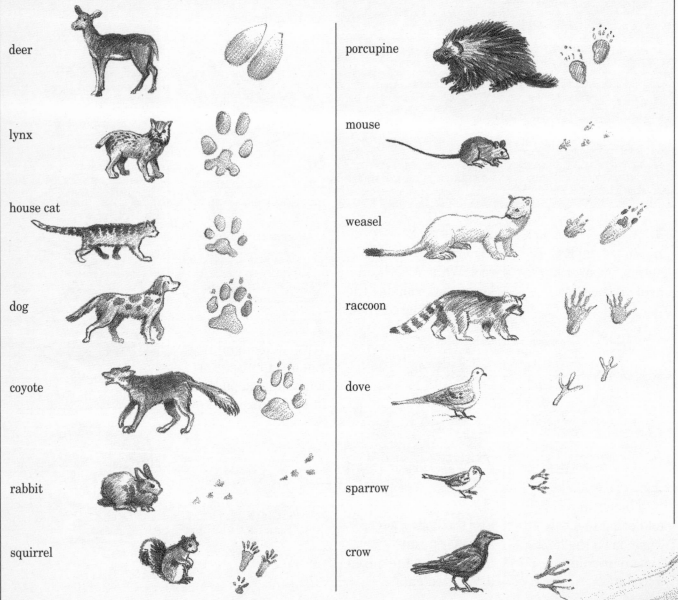

deer

lynx

house cat

dog

coyote

rabbit

squirrel

porcupine

mouse

weasel

raccoon

dove

sparrow

crow

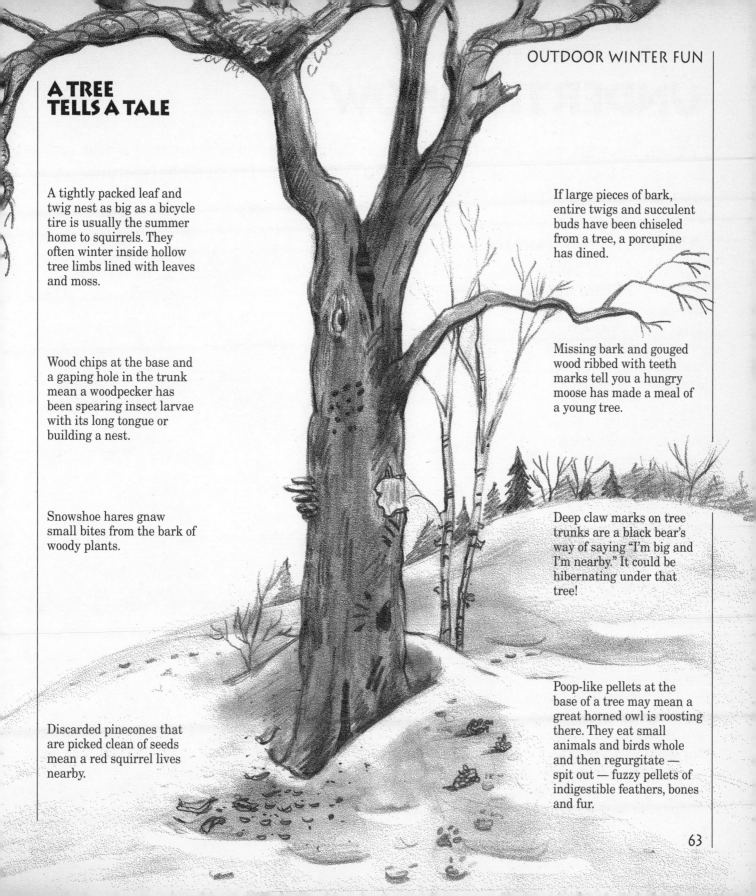

A TREE TELLS A TALE

A tightly packed leaf and twig nest as big as a bicycle tire is usually the summer home to squirrels. They often winter inside hollow tree limbs lined with leaves and moss.

Wood chips at the base and a gaping hole in the trunk mean a woodpecker has been spearing insect larvae with its long tongue or building a nest.

Snowshoe hares gnaw small bites from the bark of woody plants.

Discarded pinecones that are picked clean of seeds mean a red squirrel lives nearby.

If large pieces of bark, entire twigs and succulent buds have been chiseled from a tree, a porcupine has dined.

Missing bark and gouged wood ribbed with teeth marks tell you a hungry moose has made a meal of a young tree.

Deep claw marks on tree trunks are a black bear's way of saying "I'm big and I'm nearby." It could be hibernating under that tree!

Poop-like pellets at the base of a tree may mean a great horned owl is roosting there. They eat small animals and birds whole and then regurgitate — spit out — fuzzy pellets of indigestible feathers, bones and fur.

63

UNDER THE SNOW

When you walk with a dog through freshly fallen snow, does it burrow its nose in for a sniff? Did you know that it smells mice, voles, weasels and other creatures that live under the blanket of snow?

ATTRACTING WILDLIFE

To find out what's active under the snow, lure creatures to the surface with a little food. Place some birdseed or bread crumbs beside a sheltered spot, such as a low bush, where you have a good view from a window. On warm days chipmunks, mice, red squirrels and voles will pack their cheek pouches with food and scurry below the snow again.

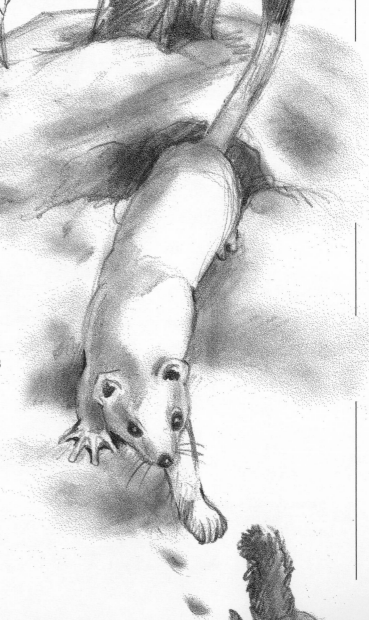

TERROR OF THE SNOWBANK

Deep snow protects many creatures from weather, but it doesn't stop predators from stalking them for food. The fierce weasel tunnels under the snow, stunning mice or other small rodents with a high-pitched screech. A lunge to the throat finishes the kill. After devouring the prey, the weasel can move in, taking over its victim's burrow. They insulate their homes with fur plucked from their prey.

   Many carnivores that live above the snow — fox, coyote, wolves, lynx, bobcats and wolverines — can smell a meal under the snow. They try to scare out their prey by jumping on top of the burrows or by digging into the snow.

TRAILS OF SPRING

In a meadow, the last snow to melt in the spring is under the hard-packed tunnels used by creatures under the snow. If you look closely, you'll find that the tunnels lead to the remains of winter burrows. Look for milkweed fluff, tufts of fur, dried grasses, droppings and footprints in the mud. Turn to page 62 to identify the footprints of the creature that wintered there.

CAMOUFLAGE

Some predators, such as weasels and arctic fox, change color in winter so they can sneak up on their prey unseen. Prey species, such as snowshoe hares or ptarmigan, turn white making it harder for them to be seen.

HOOTS, YIPS AND HOWLS

Step outside on a winter's night and listen. If you hear an owl, coyote or a wolf calling, return the call using the same sounds and rhythms. Sometimes you'll get an answer. It could be the most amazing conversation of your life!

OWL HOOTS

Most owls mate in winter. Scientists believe they stake out territories around their nests with hoots. If an owl hears you hooting, it may think you are an intruding owl and hoot back. What that hoot probably means is "get lost, this is my place."

- A great horned owl makes a series of deep hoots:

  WhaWhaWha-Whoo-Whoo
  WhaWhaWha-Whoo-Whoo

- A barred owl's hoots follow the rhythm:

  "Who cooks for you? Who cooks for you all?"
  Who Who, Who Whooo; Who Who, Whoo Hooaw

- A screech owl starts with a high quavering note and then wails down a scale to finally hold the lowest ghostly note for several seconds:

  OOOoooooooo-oo-oo-oo-oo-oooooo

- A long-eared owl's wild call can sound like a scream in the forest:

  Waaaaaaaaaaaaaaaaaaaaaaaaaaaaaaaaa

COYOTE YIPS AND WOLF HOWLS

Scientists think coyotes and wolves call to locate pack members, stake out territory, announce a hunt or simply for the fun of it. Sometimes when one calls, another responds; sometimes the whole pack will sing in chorus.

If you're lucky enough to hear a whole chorus, listen carefully. When the calls are all "yips" it's a coyote pack. But if you're in the wilderness and hear howls among the yips — Ah . . . Oooooo . . . Ooooo — you're hearing timber wolves. Try to yip or howl back. Sometimes a coyote or wolf will answer. But once it senses you're human, it will leave. Healthy wild animals are afraid of people. If a wild animal ever approaches you, leave immediately. It may be sick or injured and dangerous.

WINTER BIRD FEEDING

Get to know the winter birds in your area by feeding them. If you offer a variety of foods, you'll attract and get to know different species.

SITING BIRD FEEDERS

Birds need to feel safe when feeding. Place feeders at least 3 m (10 ft.) from a window and where there is shelter. Make sure the feeder is out of reach of any dogs or cats.

BELL FEEDER

Keep a ready supply of these bell feeders in the freezer. It's time to put out a new one when a squirrel runs away with the walnut.

You'll need:
50 mL (¼ cup) peanut butter
50 mL (¼ cup) lard or bacon dripping
50 mL (¼ cup) sunflower seeds
50 mL (¼ cup) mixed birdseed
a large bowl
a wooden spoon
a clean tin can
string
a walnut in the shell
scissors
a can opener

1.

Combine the peanut butter, lard or bacon dripping, sunflower seeds and birdseed in a large bowl with a wooden spoon. Place one spoonful in the bottom of the can.

2.

Cut a piece of string about 60 cm (2 ft.) long. Tie the string around the walnut and wedge the nut in the middle of the peanut butter mixture in the bottom of the can.

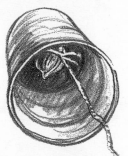

3.

Fill the can with the rest of the mixture, gently pulling the string up through the middle of the can as you fill it. Pat the mixture down with a spoon.

4.

Place the can in the freezer for several hours until the mixture is very hard.

5.

With an adult's help open the bottom of the can with the can opener and carefully discard the lid. Push the frozen contents out of the can being careful not to cut yourself on the can.

6.

Hang your bell feeder outdoors on a cold day from a tree branch, fence post or a bird feeder. If the weather turns mild, the mixture may fall to the ground where ground-feeding birds will find it.

SUET FEEDER

Many birds need fat in their winter diet to help keep them warm. Ask the butcher at the store for a large piece of beef suet. Place it in an onion bag, tying the bag closed with string or a twist tie. Hang it outside and watch for woodpeckers, chickadees, nuthatches and other hungry birds.

CRASHES

Birds sometimes crash into windows, recover and fly away. To help prevent this, make a black silhouette cutout of a hawk using construction paper or shelf liner and stick it to one corner of the window.

FEEDING SQUIRRELS

If it's called a bird feeder, why is it full of squirrels? Your challenge, should you choose to accept it, is to prevent numerous and greedy squirrels from taking all the feed from the birds. It might be an impossible mission.

RECORD BAFFLES

Use old, scratched or warped long-playing records to slow down squirrels. See how long it takes them to beat the record.

You'll need:
plastic-coated clothesline wire
wire clippers or a hacksaw
pliers
4 records
a hanging bird feeder

1.

With an adult's help, choose a site between two fence posts, deck posts, pillars or trees where the clothesline can hang 2 m (6½ ft.) off the ground and away from overhanging branches.

2.

With wire cutters, cut the amount of line you'll need, leaving extra for tying knots.

3.

Tie one end of the line to a post, pillar or tree. Tug the knot tight with pliers.

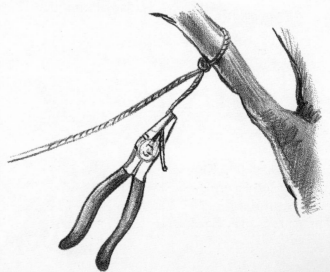

4.

Tie a loose knot about 1 m (1 yd.) to one side of where you want to hang the feeder. Slide a record on the line and tie another knot close to the record. Leave a space of 50 cm (20 in.) and tie another knot. Slide on a second record and tie another knot. Continue until all four records are knotted in place on the line.

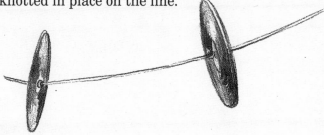

5.

Secure the loose end of the line around the second post, tightening the knot with pliers.

6.

Fill the bird feeder with seed and hang it between two records. See how long it takes for the squirrels to investigate.

SQUIRREL FEEDERS

If you can't beat 'em, feed 'em. Provide squirrels with their favorite foods, and they might leave the birds' food alone.

- With an adult's help, cut a coconut in half with a handsaw. Drink or pour out the milk. Using a sharp nail, make a hole on either side of the coconut. From the inside of the coconut, thread a knotted piece of string through each hole. Fill with a mixture of equal portions of birdseed and peanut butter. The squirrels will gnaw out the coconut meat too.

- When a plastic peanut butter jar is almost empty, place the jar under the feeder and watch the squirrels go to work. Before long, the jar will be licked and pawed clean. Then you can recycle the jar.

IN AND UNDER THE ICE

When a pond is covered in ice, it's hard to believe that anything is alive and moving underneath. But there is. Here's how you can find out for yourself. Take an adult with you and don't walk out on the ice.

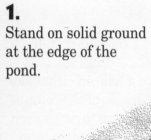

You'll need:

a hatchet

a white-bottomed, large plastic bucket such as an ice cream container

1.
Stand on solid ground at the edge of the pond.

2.
Ask an adult to chop a hole through the ice down to the water below.

3.
Fill the plastic container with the chips of ice and ice-cold water.

4.
Carry the container inside and observe it over several weeks.

The ice water may look clear and cold, but it's full of tiny eggs and creatures that will develop in the spring-like warmth of your house. Over the weeks, they will live through several generations — some will grow and be eaten by (or eat) others that emerge. Check every day and watch the drama unfold. Here's what to look for.

Creatures that are longer than 1 cm ($\frac{1}{2}$ in.):

- fairy shrimp

- alderfly larva

- phantom midge

- scud or freshwater shrimp

Creatures that are shorter than 1 cm ($\frac{1}{2}$ in.):

- cyclops

- daphnia or water flea

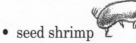

- seed shrimp

- water mite

- springtails or snow fleas

BLACK ICE

Sometimes the ice on a pond freezes so quickly it's thick but clear as glass. On those unusual occasions, you can stand on the land beside the pond and look through ice to the black bottom. Under the ice, look for fish, tadpoles and turtles swimming along as if it were summer. You may even see frogs, beetles, mussels and other creatures partly dug into the bottom where they spend the winter.

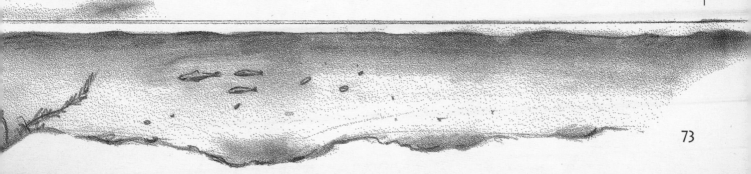

INDOOR WINTER FUN

Wintertime fun doesn't stop when you move indoors. Why not continue the winter theme by making a mobile of string snowflakes or creating a blizzard in a jar? You may decide to carve a winter's scene in scrimshaw or make a memory book to record your winter traditions. Then join friends for a rousing card or board game. Even when you are snowed in, there is so much to do!

CROKINOLE

Can you dodge obstacles, scatter opponents and hit the winning jackpot with only the flick of a finger? Test your skills in the crazy game of crokinole. You can even make your own crokinole board.

You'll need:

4 75 cm (30 in.) squares of sturdy cardboard
a 30 cm (1 ft.) length of string attached to a pencil
scissors or a craft knife
a measuring tape
12 checker disks of one color and 12 of another
white glue
a black marker
8 sturdy thumbtacks

1.
Cut the corners off one square of cardboard to make an eight-sided figure. This will be your crokinole board base.

2.
With your thumb, hold the end of the string on the midpoint of a second cardboard square. Pull the pencil so the string is tight and draw a circle with a radius of the full 30 cm (1 ft.) of the string.

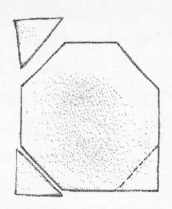

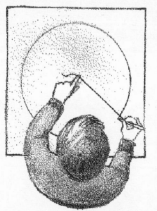

3.
Cut out the circle and then cut two more from the remaining cardboard pieces.

4.
Cut a hole, just larger than a checker disk, in the center of the three cardboard circles.

5.
Glue the circles together and then glue them onto the middle of your base piece. Weigh down the board with a heavy object while the glue dries.

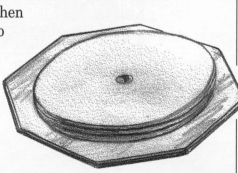

6.

Draw three more circles with the string and pencil on the top piece of cardboard from the midpoint. The radius of the first circle should be 28 cm (11½ in.), the second 20 cm (8 in.), and the third 10 cm (4 in.). Go over the lines with marker.

7.

Place the eight tacks evenly around the smallest drawn circle.

8.

With the marker, write the number 20 in the hole, 15 in the ring between the hole and the tacks, 10 outside the tacks and 5 in the outside ring.

9.

The outside line is the starting line. Draw four evenly spaced lines from it, across the ring valued 5, to the next line. These are called quadrant lines.

CROKINOLE RULES

With two players, each starts with 12 checker disks of one color. Players sit opposite each other and take turns shooting their disks.

- Place a disk on the starting line inside the quadrant facing you. Hold your middle finger under your thumb and flick it to shoot the disk forward. Once the game starts, players cannot change places or move the board.

- The object of the game is to shoot your disks into high-scoring positions and knock your opponent's disks into low-scoring ones or out altogether. When a disk lands in the hole, it is removed but counts as 20.

- At the end of each round, players add up their scores. Disks touching lines take the lower value. Disks on the starting line are out. Rounds are played until a player reaches 100 points.

- With four players, each starts with 6 checkers. Make two teams with team members facing one another. Play moves clockwise around the table.

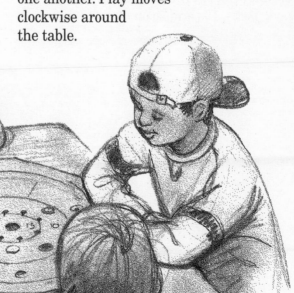

DONKEY

The object of this card game is to become the president. Then it's up to the other players to topple the president from power. All you need is a full deck of cards with jokers and three or more players.

PLAYING THE FIRST ROUND

1.

Choose a dealer by cutting the deck. The person who turns over the highest card shuffles and deals out the entire deck.

3.

The dealer starts play by laying down a card or cards of his choice. If he has four of a kind (four 3s, for example), he starts with that. Other players follow, in a clockwise manner, playing four of a kind of a greater value than the person before them or they pass.

2.

Players sort their hand in value order, with jokers highest, followed by 2s, aces, kings, queens, jacks, 10s and so on down to 3s.

4.

In play:

- a joker beats any lead, including four of a kind

- two 2s beat three or four of a kind, but not a joker

- one 2 beats two of a kind or any lead lower than 2

5.

The last player, who is able to follow the dealer's lead, leads next with three or two of a kind, or any card of her choosing. Continue playing until a player is out of cards. She becomes the president.

6.

The player to the left of the president leads, and play continues until another player is out of cards. This person is called the vice president.

7.

The player to the left of the vice president leads next. Continue until all players are out of cards. Any players to finish after the vice president are called clerks, but the last person to get rid of his cards is called the donkey.

PLAYING THE REST OF THE GAME

1.

The president shuffles the deck. The person to her left cuts the cards. Then the president deals out the entire deck.

2.

Players sort their cards by value. Before play begins, the donkey gives his two best cards to the president and the president gives the donkey two cards of her choice, usually low cards. The lowest clerk gives the vice president her highest card and the vice president gives the clerk a card of his choice, usually the lowest. When there are three players, only the president and donkey exchange cards.

SNOW STRUCTURES

Take on a winter construction challenge — you won't need a hard hat when you're building with mini-marshmallows and toothpicks.

✳ ✳

S N O W F L A K E S

Every snowflake is slightly different, depending on the conditions under which it formed and fell. But all snowflakes have six points.
To make a classic snowflake structure:

1.

Start with one marshmallow. Poke six toothpicks into the marshmallow to look like spokes.

2.

Poke a marshmallow onto the end of each toothpick.

3.

Connect the six marshmallows in a circle with toothpicks.

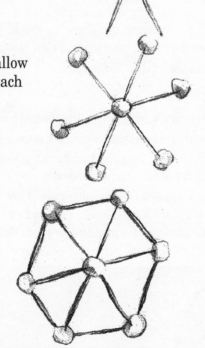

4.

Poke a toothpick into each of the marshmallows in the circle, pointing away from the center, and tip the toothpick ends with marshmallows.

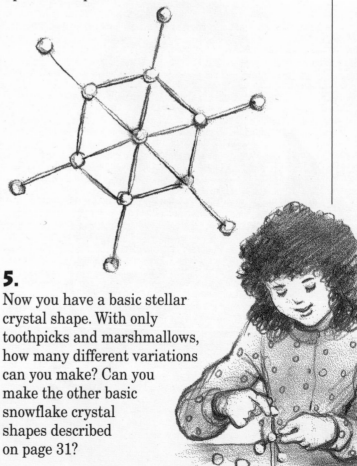

5.

Now you have a basic stellar crystal shape. With only toothpicks and marshmallows, how many different variations can you make? Can you make the other basic snowflake crystal shapes described on page 31?

MALLOW DOMES

1.

Make a triangle with three toothpicks. Hold the shape by poking the toothpicks into marshmallows at the three points of the triangle.

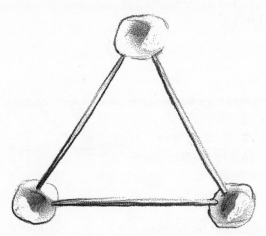

2.

Add three more toothpick and marshmallow triangles, each sharing one side with the original triangle as shown. With ten triangles connected this way, you can form a dome.

3.

Now, challenge yourself to make a dome that starts with one five-sided toothpick and marshmallow figure, or pentagon. Add five more pentagons, each sharing one side with your first pentagon. Keep adding pentagons until you have made a dome.

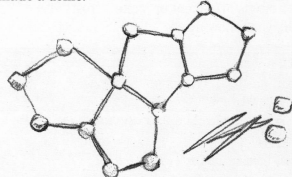

4.

The final challenge — construct a dome with six-sided marshmallow and toothpick figures, or hexagons.

BLIZZARDS AND ICICLES

Bring the wildest winter weather indoors, even if there are no flurries in the forecast. Shake up a blizzard with a snow dome and hang icicles from the window.

SNOW DOME

Use a single ornament or make a frosty scene inside your snow dome.

You'll need:
a clean, small jar with a tight-fitting lid (a baby food jar works well)
a seasonal ornament or plastic figurine
waterproof glue
a glass measuring cup or jug
water
glitter or tiny pieces of aluminum foil

1.
Using a generous amount of glue, stick the ornament to the middle of the inside of the jar lid, leaving space to screw the lid onto the jar. Allow the glue to dry thoroughly.

2.
Completely cover the bottom of the jar with a layer of glitter or bits of aluminum foil.

3.
Fill the glass measuring cup with water and allow the water to sit until it is clear. Slowly fill the jar with water.

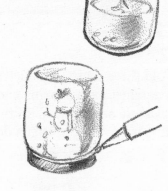

4.
Screw the lid onto the jar and tighten. Turn the jar lid side down and run a bead of glue between the lid and the glass. Allow the glue to dry for several hours.

5.
Shake the dome and watch the snow flurries swirl around the ornament.

ICICLES INDOORS

Hang these crystal icicles inside a window frame and send sun sparkles through your home.

You'll need:
a paper clip
30 cm (1 ft.) yarn
a pencil
a tall, clean jar
hot water
borax (a natural laundry and cleaning product)
a long-handled spoon or stir stick

1.

Attach a paper clip to one end of the yarn and wind the other end around a pencil.

2.

Fill the jar with hot water. For every cup of water, add 50 mL (1/4 cup) of borax. Stir to dissolve as much of the borax as possible.

3.

Place the pencil across the mouth of the jar so one end of the yarn dangles down into the solution but the paper clip does not quite touch the bottom.

4.

Leave undisturbed for 24 hours. Pull the crystal-covered yarn out of the solution and hang to dry. Remove the paper clip. Display your crystal icicle in a sunny window.

STRING SNOWFLAKES

Make string snowflakes and hang them from a tree or place them around the plastic socket of festive winter lights. Tie them to a branch to make a mobile.

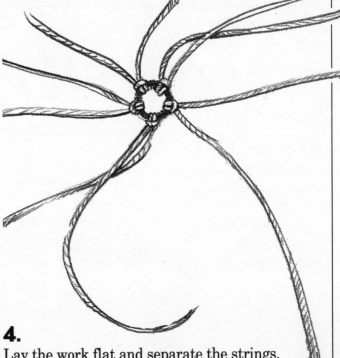

You'll need:
white pipe cleaners
white kitchen string
scissors
hairspray (CFC-free) or spray starch
newsprint
glitter (optional)

1.
Cut a 5 cm (2 in.) piece of pipe cleaner. Form it into a ring and twist the ends together.

2.
Cut five 30 cm. (12 in.) pieces of string and fold each in half.

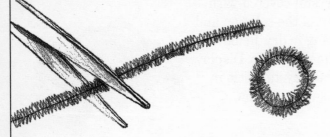

3.
Place the looped end of one string under the pipe cleaner ring. Pull the loose ends of the string through the loop and tighten around the ring. Attach the remaining four strings evenly around the ring.

4.
Lay the work flat and separate the strings.

5.

Create a pattern of knots using a square, or reef, knot. Start with two strings side by side that originate from different looped strings. Working near the ring, pick up the left-hand string. Pass it over the right string, back under and over the top again. The end of the left-hand string is now on the right of the work.

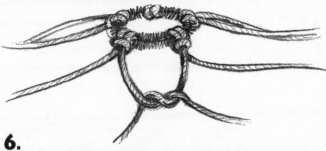

6.

Pick up the end of the original right-hand string (now on the left) and place it over, under and over the original left-hand string close to the ring. Gently pull the two ends and tighten the knot about 1.5 cm (⁵⁄₈ in.) from the ring.

7.

Repeat steps 5 to 7 until there are five knots 1.5 cm (⁵⁄₈ in.) from the ring. Make five more knots 1.5 cm (⁵⁄₈ in.) away from the first set of knots. Finish with five knots 1.5 cm (⁵⁄₈ in.) from the second set of knots.

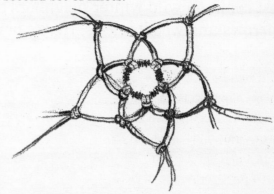

8.

Trim the excess string 1 cm (¹⁄₂ in.) from the last knots. Fray the ends of the strings.

9.

Place the completed snowflake on a piece of newsprint and spray thoroughly with hairspray. Dust some snowflakes with glitter while wet with hairspray, if desired. Allow to dry.

WINTER MASKS

Northern people admire bears, wolves, ravens, owls and deer. Ancient northerners believed a human could absorb a wild animal's strengths by wearing its mask. Your most common wild winter neighbors are probably birds — hardy chickadees, jays, sparrows and woodpeckers. Here's how you can make a bird mask.

You'll need:
2 sheets of paper and a pencil
a cardboard box (a shoebox or cereal box work well)
scissors, glue, masking tape
paints and a paintbrush
colored paper or scraps of cloth
2 pieces of string, about 60 cm (2 ft.) long

1.

Place a sheet of paper on your face and carefully mark your eyes and nose.

2.

On a table and with a pencil, draw a mask pattern around the eyes, across the cheeks and over the middle of the nose as shown. (This pattern does not cover the nostrils, mouth or chin.) Cut out your pattern.

3.

Fold the pattern in half at the nose and trim the halves so the two eyepieces mirror each other.

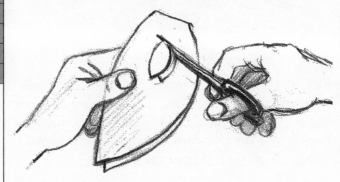

4.

Place the pattern on the box so the fold at the nose lies along one edge of the box as shown. Trace the pattern on the sides and cut out the cardboard mask.

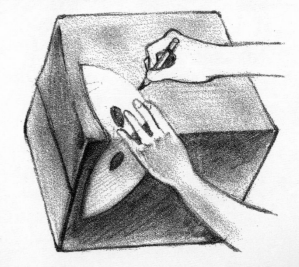

5.

Now create the beak. If you are making a specific bird, consult a bird guide to learn the curve of its beak. Fold the second piece of paper in half, draw and cut out a side-view beak pattern along the fold. Place the fold on an edge of the cardboard box, trace the outline of the pattern on two sides of the box and cut out the cardboard beak.

6.

Glue and tape the cardboard beak, from the inside, onto the face of the cardboard mask.

7.

Paint the beak and eyes to look like your bird.

8.

Cut out feathers from colored paper and/or scraps of cloth. Start gluing these feathers at the outside edge of the mask and work toward the beak. For a natural effect, place each cut-out feather you glue down to cover the base of the feather before.

9.

Tape the two lengths of string to the sides of the mask so you can tie it on at the back of your head.

WINTER SPIRITS

Ancestors of the Inuit people from eastern Siberia, Alaska, Canada and Greenland carved masks of the spirits of winter and severe weather. Can you imagine the face of a terrible winter storm and then turn that into a mask?

SCRIMSHAW

In past times on cold winter nights at sea, sailors liked to while the time away by carving scenes from their travels into whalebones, whale teeth or walrus tusks. This folk art was called scrimshaw from the word "scrimshanker," or "time-waster," in sailor's slang. Try your hand at the craft of scrimshaw.

You'll need:
a paper and pencil
a cutting board
a large bar of soft white soap
a knife (a dinner knife will do for soap carving)
washable paint and a paintbrush
a wet cloth

1.

Plan your design on paper with a pencil. Traditional scrimshaw shows scenes from arctic lands and whaling, but modern scrimshankers draw scenes from stories about anything from picnics to dragons.

2.

Place your bar of soap on the cutting board. Stroking your knife away from you, scrape off the brand name or any other writing on the soap.

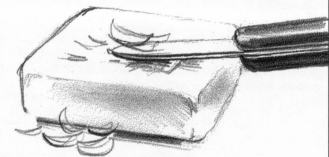

3.

Copy your design into the soap by carefully cutting with the knife. Smooth the edges of the bar to make the whole piece attractive.

4.

With your paintbrush tip, paint the lines you carved. In traditional scrimshaw, sailors used only the color black, but today artists use many colors. Keep the paint inside the cut lines on the soap.

5.

After the paint has dried, remove any splotches that dropped outside the carved lines with the wet cloth and the knife.

STORYKNIVES

On both the Alaskan and Siberian shores of the Bering Sea, Yupik girls play a traditional game in which they share stories without talking. Instead, they draw their stories in the snow or ice with storyknives. The handles and blades of the storyknives are usually decorated with scrimshaw carvings of scenes from their favorite tales.

RUG HOOKING

Is there a spot where your bare feet always meet the cold floor? Beside the bed? Near the fireplace? Hooking is an ancient craft that recycles old fabric into warm mats. Here's how to hook a colorful mat to cover the cold spots in your floor.

You'll need:

masking tape

a 50 cm (20 in.) square of open weave burlap (available at craft supply stores)

a pencil, paper and scissors

a permanent marker

an embroidery hoop (about 36 cm or 14 in. across) or a heavy book

40 cm (16 in.) strips of washed material such as wool flannel, cut or ripped 0.5 cm (1/4 in.) wide
OR T-shirt cotton, cut or ripped 1 cm (1/2 in.) wide and then stretched until the edges curl
OR panty hose, cut around the leg 2.5 cm (1 in.) wide and stretched

a hook with a wooden handle or a crochet hook (available at craft supply stores)

a needle and polyester thread

1.
Tape around the edges of the burlap, with masking tape.

2.
With pencil and paper, plan the design that you want to hook. Decide on the colors based on the fabric available. Copy your final design onto the burlap with permanent marker. Each area where you want a different color should be outlined in marker.

3.
Place the burlap, pattern side up, into your hoop or put one edge of the burlap under a heavy book on a table and pull the burlap toward you.

4.
Hold the hook in your writing hand with the barb facing up. Hold a strip of fabric with your other hand against the underside of the burlap.

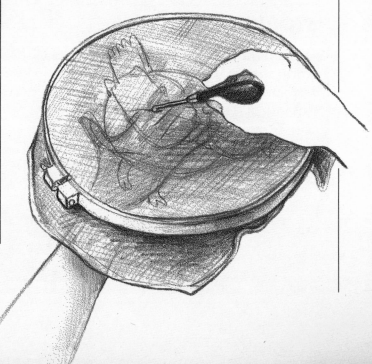

5.

Poke the hook down through the burlap. Pull the end of the fabric strip up through to the top until it sticks up about 2 cm (³/₄ in.).

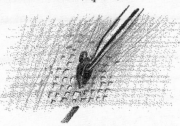

6.

Skip two holes in the burlap, poke the hook down again and pull a loop of fabric up through the burlap to the height 0.5 cm (¹/₄ in.). Take out your hook and leave the loop sitting on top of the burlap, squeezed in place by the burlap threads under it.

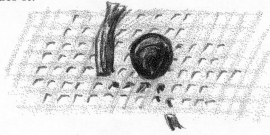

7.

Work either left or right in a line. Skip two more holes, poke your hook in again, pull up the fabric from below making another loop beside the first. Keep repeating. All your loops should be about the same size. There should be no burlap showing between the loops on the topside. On the underside, the fabric should lie flat.

8.

When you get to the end of a fabric strip or want to change color, hook the fabric strip up through the burlap so the end is on the topside and snip it off at loop height. Start the next strip or color as in step 5 through the same hole in the burlap and continue to hook as in steps 6 and 7.

9.

When the burlap is covered in loops, remove the masking tape, fold excess burlap to the back and sew flat with a needle and polyester thread.

PAPER CRAFTS

Decorate for a party or special event by looping paper snow-people or paper chains around door frames, windows or a tree. Then create an indoor snowstorm with lots of snowflake cutouts fluttering from the window!

PAPER SNOW-PEOPLE

You'll need:

a ruler
white paper 22 cm x 27 cm (8½ in. x 11 in.)
a pencil
scissors
markers
a glue stick

1.
Fold the paper into three 9 cm (3½ in.) sections, pressing firmly along the fold lines.

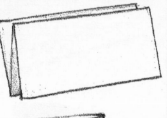

2.
Draw a three-ball snowman. The top ball forms the head and hat and does not touch the folds. The middle ball is slightly larger, with the arms extending through the folds. The lower ball is the full width of the paper at its widest point.

3.
Cut out the hat and head. Cut out the rest of the snowman without cutting where the arms and lowest ball touch the sides.

4.
Leave the snowman white or use markers to decorate with a face, buttons and a scarf.

5.
Make more snow-people and join them all together at the arms with a dab of glue.

PAPER CHAINS

You'll need:

white paper

scissors

a glue stick

1.
Cut pieces of paper into 5 cm (2 in.) strips. Fold in half, lengthwise.

2.
Cut out triangles of various sizes along the fold, the full length of the strip. Leave a small space between each triangle. Unfold and press flat.

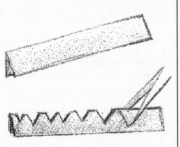

3.
Form one strip of paper into a circle, held together with a dab of glue at the end. Loop the next strip through the circle before gluing. Continue until the chain is the desired length. If you hang it near a window, the light will shine through the crystal-like patterns in the chain.

SNOWFLAKE CUTOUTS

You'll need:

white paper

scissors

white thread

tape

1.
Cut a circle of paper with a diameter of 13 cm (5 in.).

2.
Fold in half three times. Cut small triangles, circles and other designs along all sides of the paper.

3.
Unfold and press flat. Tape a piece of thread to the edge of the snowflake and tape the thread to the window frame, or tie to a tree branch.

DREAM CATCHER

According to Navajo legend, all dreams float in the night air. A dream catcher, swinging freely above a sleeping person, traps bad dreams in its web. Good dreams slip through the hole in the center and slide down the feather to the sleeper.

You'll need:
a small plastic ring from below the cap of a jug or plastic bottle (a thin piece of willow tied in a circle will work, too)
1 m (3 ft.) thin, plastic craft string
scissors
waxed dental floss
seed beads and jumbo seed beads
2 feathers

1.

Tie the string around the plastic ring with a single knot. Working in a clockwise direction, wind the string around the ring until reaching the knot. Do not overlap the string. Untie the knot and hold in place with one hand. Continue to wind the string around the ring until there is no ring showing. Tie the two ends of string together with a double knot. Trim any remaining string.

2.

Count the number of times the string looped around the ring — for example, 48 times. Tie 1 m (3 ft.) of dental floss to the ring where the string is knotted. Then make eight loops around the inside of the ring. Work clockwise and count six loops of string from the knot. Leave a small amount of slack and then wind the floss around the ring twice. Repeat until you are back at the beginning. There should be eight loops.

3.

For the next round, hold the end of the floss as if it were a needle and thread. Thread a few beads onto the floss for each of the following loops.

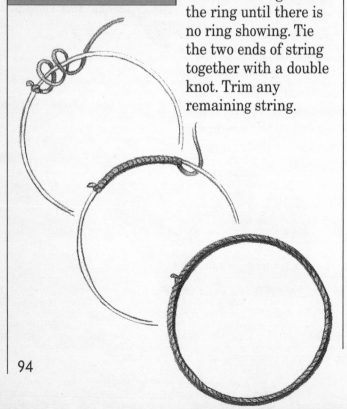

4.

Bring the floss up and through the first loop and pull until taut. Repeat to form a double knot. Take the thread behind the next loop and repeat this process for all eight loops.

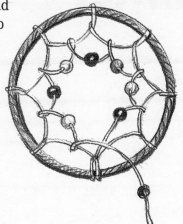

5.

Continue adding to the web in this manner until there is a small hole left in the center. Tie off the floss by knotting it around a large bead.

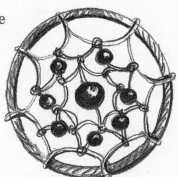

6.

Fold a 60 cm (2 ft.) piece of floss in half. Slip the folded end under the outside ring. Form a knot by slipping the other end of the floss through the folded end and tighten. This floss is for hanging the dream catcher.

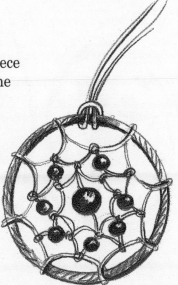

7.

Knot a large bead to one end of a 15 cm (6 in.) piece of dental floss. Thread on a second large bead. Thread 5 cm (2 in.) of the floss with seed beads.

8.

Run a bead of glue along the shaft of a feather and slide up into the two large beads. Allow to dry. Make a second feather-and-bead string and tie them both to the ring opposite the hang-up floss.

9.

Hang the dream catcher near your bed. Pleasant dreams.

If you can't complete the craft in one sitting, hold the string in place on the ring with a small piece of tape. Remove the tape to finish the craft.

CHARMS AND CHIMES

ICE CHARMS

On cold, clear days, sunlight sparkles off ice. Bring that sparkle close to home by hanging pretty ice charms outside your windows.

You'll need:

several shallow pie plates or baking pans of assorted shapes

water

1 m (3 ft.) lengths of colorful yarn

thin slices of orange, lemon or lime

small evergreen branches

wild winter berries

1.
Fill each pan with water to just below the rim.

2.
Circle the inside of each pan with a length of yarn so the yarn gets wet and sinks. Drape the ends of the yarn over the rim and out of the water.

3.
Place fruit slices, greenery and berries in the water inside the yarn circle. Put only a few items in each pan — the clear, empty spaces make the sparkle effect.

4.
When it's below freezing, put the pans outside on a flat surface.

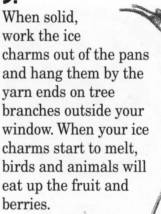

5.
When solid, work the ice charms out of the pans and hang them by the yarn ends on tree branches outside your window. When your ice charms start to melt, birds and animals will eat up the fruit and berries.

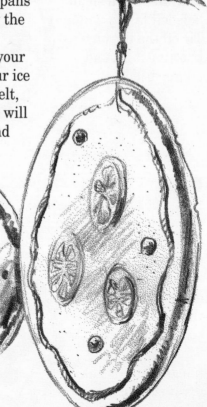

WIND CHIMES

Sometimes you can collect driftwood and shells in winter along the shore of an ocean or a big lake. Do some beachcombing to collect pieces to make wind chimes.

You'll need:

a circle of wood about 0.5 cm (¼ in.) thick and 10 cm (4 in.) across

a hand drill and small bit

string

scissors

white glue

driftwood pieces and light shells, 5 to 8 cm (2 to 3 in.) long

1.

Ask an adult to help you drill nine small holes around the wood circle.

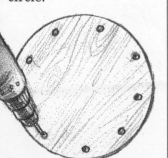

2.

Tie a piece of string 30 cm (1 ft.) long into every third hole. Tie the free end of these strings all together in a double knot. You'll hang the finished product from this knot.

3.

The other six holes are for hanging your chime pieces. Attach strings that dangle down from these holes. The strings don't need to be the same length.

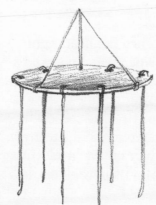

4.

Tie or glue on driftwood and shells to the chime strings.

5.

Hang your wind chimes in a place where there is a breeze so the pieces will tap each other and chime.

97

WINTER GREENS

This crazy planter will green up your winter and is guaranteed to make everyone laugh.

You'll need:

scissors

an old pair of panty hose

a lightbulb

buttons, a needle and thread

permanent marker

grass seed — ryegrass grows fastest

potting soil

a small dish or cup

1.

Cut one leg off a pair of panty hose 30 cm (1 ft.) up from the foot.

2.

Put the lightbulb inside the toe to stretch the fabric. By drawing with markers and sewing on buttons, make a face on the panty hose (the tip of the toe is the top of the head). Remove the lightbulb.

3.

Put several spoonfuls of the grass seed into the toe followed by a few cups of potting soil. Tie a knot in the panty hose to hold the soil and seed in a tight ball at the toe end.

4.

Turn the head right side up and place on a small dish or cup. Water daily. In a week or two, the seeds will sprout and make green hair on the head. Give it a trim when needed.

WINTER BLOOMS

You can do some winter gardening by tricking spring flowers into blooming.

You'll need:

5 or 6 bulbs — crocus, tulip, daffodil, narcissus or hyacinth

a medium-shallow dish or pie plate

pebbles

1.

Six weeks before you want flowers, place the bulbs pointed-side up in the dish or pie plate. The bulbs should not touch each other.

2.

Cover the bulbs with pebbles up to, but not over, the shoot tips.

3.

Half fill the dish or plate with water and place it in a dark cupboard. Whenever the dish bottom dries, add more water.

4.

When the shoots start to grow, bring the dish or pie plate out into daylight. Add fresh water twice a week until the blooms are all finished.

WINTERGREEN

Some plants stay green even through the winter. Holly, which pokes out greenly from under the snow, was once thought to keep away evil spirits. Evergreen boughs hung over doors and windows were believed to keep away illness. One wild woodland plant is actually called wintergreen. Many people believe it has important healing powers.

MEMORY BOOK

Keep the winter season alive all year long in a personalized scrapbook. Use it to record your favorite activities, stories, storms and family "firsts." Leave space for winter guests to sign their names and write comments on their visits. Keep your memory book in a handy spot where it can be read, enjoyed and added to.

You'll need:
2 covers made from cardboard 23 cm x 30 cm (9 in. x 12 in.)
fallen birchbark (optional)
white glue, scissors, markers, a ruler, a pencil
20 lined and 8 unlined 22 cm x 27 cm (8½ in. x 11 in.) three-holed sheets of white paper
paper reinforcements
4 sheets of construction paper, 22 cm x 27 cm (8½ in. x 11 in.)
a one-hole punch
3 large "O" rings

1.

Center a piece of three-holed paper on the inside of a cover and use the one-hole punch to make three matching holes down the right side of this top cover. Repeat to make three holes down the left side of the bottom cover.

2.

Decorate the front and back covers with birchbark, drawings or photographs.

3.

Using the one-hole punch and a piece of three-holed paper, make three holes in each piece of construction paper.

4.

Divide the white paper into four piles of four lined and two unlined sheets. Top each pile with a piece of construction paper as a section divider.

6.

Gather everything into one stack of paper. Place the front cover on top of the stack. Place the back cover on the bottom. Hold the book together with three "O" rings.

5.

Attach reinforcements to all the sheets of paper.

7.

Write the title of the section (guests, wild visitors, special events, games and so on) and decorate each section divider. Use the lined paper for written records and the unlined paper for drawings or glued-in mementos. Add more paper or sections as needed.

CELEBRATE WINTER

Turn the winter season into one long fun-filled celebration. Whether you're celebrating Christmas, Chanukah, Kwanzaa, New Year's, a special birthday or just being together, jazz up the festivities with edible decorations, including your own unique gingerbread house. Tap a maple tree and serve up a plate of pancakes slathered with syrup. Prepare a spectacular Olympic Day for neighbors, friends and family. Cap it off with a frosty outdoor medal ceremony. There's so much to do, winter isn't long enough! Remember to ask for an adult's help when using the stove or microwave. Wear thick oven mitts when handling pots and pans.

TREAT TREE

Decorate a tree branch with homemade ornaments and edible treats. Candies for the winter holidays, paper hearts for Valentine's Day and chocolate eggs for spring — the twigs will never be empty!

You'll need:
a large, bare tree branch
a clean, empty coffee can
construction or wrapping paper
yarn
ribbon
scissors
sticky tape
sand
candies, such as jellies, jujubes, wrapped chocolates and mini candy canes

1.

Look for a fallen branch, or clip a large branch from a hawthorn, black locust or any tree with a lot of small twigs. Species with thorns work well, but be careful of them.

2.

Decorate the outside of the can with colorful paper and ribbon. Fill the can with moist sand.

3.

Stick the thick end of the branch right to the bottom of the can and pat the sand tightly around the stem.

4.

Cut out construction-paper decorations and hang them on the branches with yarn.

5.

Push jellies or jujubes onto twigs and thorns. Hang candy canes from the branches. Make sure there are no bits of thorn or twig in the candy before eating it.

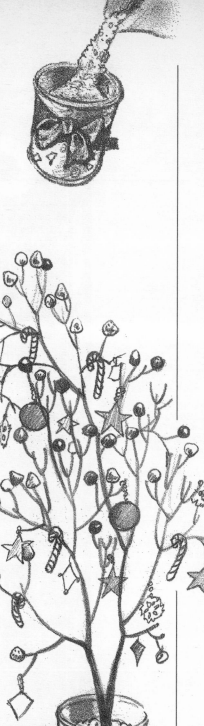

PINECONE SKIER

Hang this little skier from a tree or make several for a winter scene.

You'll need:

2 Popsicle sticks or craft sticks

glue, a craft knife

a Ping-Pong ball

permanent markers

felt

pinecones about 10 cm (4 in.) high

pipe cleaners

2 wooden skewers or twigs

1.
With an adult's help, make a pair of skis from the Popsicle or craft sticks by carving points at one end and making the other end straight across. Glue the sticks together in an "X."

2.
Draw a face with markers on the Ping-Pong ball. Glue on a small triangular felt hat.

3.
Glue the head to the flat bottom of the cone. Wrap a pipe cleaner around the neck and form a loop at the back of the skier for hanging it up.

4.
Wrap a rectangle of felt scarf around the neck and knot in place. Wrap a pipe cleaner around the cone and make small loops at the ends for the hands.

5.
Glue ski poles made from the sharp end of two skewers or small twigs to the hand loops. Slide a dime-sized circle of felt onto the end of the poles.

6.
Glue the narrow end of the cone to the sticks.

WINTER DESSERTS

Round off a winter meal with a yummy seasonal dessert.

CRISPY APPLE BAKE

You'll need:
6 large cooking apples
salt
76 mL (1/3 cup) margarine
125 mL (1/2 cup) brown sugar
125 mL (1/2 cup) oatmeal
5 mL (1 teaspoon) cinnamon
a vegetable peeler, a paring knife, a small pot
an oven proof casserole
oven mitts

1.
Preheat the oven to 180°C (350°F).

2.
Peel, core and slice the apples. Toss in a casserole with a pinch of salt.

3.
In a small pot, melt the margarine. Remove the pot from the heat and stir in the sugar, oatmeal and cinnamon.

4.
Spoon the sugar mixture on top of the apples. Bake for 45 minutes. Wearing oven mitts, remove from the oven and cool slightly before serving.

INDOOR SMORES

Here's how to make a dozen smores.

You'll need:

a cookie sheet

24 graham or chocolate wafers

12 large marshmallows

12 small pieces of chocolate

oven mitts

a hot pad

a spatula

a plate

1.
With an adult's help, place the oven rack in the highest position. Turn on the broiler.

2.
Place 12 wafers on the cookie sheet, leaving space between each wafer.

3.
Push a piece of chocolate into the middle of each marshmallow. Place one on top of each wafer.

4.
Put on, and keep on, the oven mitts. Slide the cookie sheet under the broiler. Leave the oven door open and watch the marshmallows. When they swell and turn golden brown, in about one minute, remove from the oven and place on a hot pad.

I WANT SMORE PLEASE

5.
Cool for a minute before covering each marshmallow with another wafer. Lift the smores onto a serving plate.

'WAVED SMORES

Place chocolate digestive cookies topped with marshmallows onto a microwave-proof plate. Microwave on high for 8 seconds. Remove from the oven and cover each treat with another wafer. Cool slightly and enjoy.

GINGERBREAD HOUSE

Make a gingerbread house, and then show it off to family and friends.
The gingerbread will taste fresh even after several weeks,
but this recipe is so yummy it may not last that long.

DESIGNING YOUR HOUSE

Draw the walls and roof to size on cardboard. Cut out and
assemble to be sure the pieces all fit together. Be creative —
make a simple version of your own house, a church, a space
station, a monster's lair or whatever else is fun for you. Save
the cardboard pieces to use as stencils for cutting out the
dough. Here's a sample design:

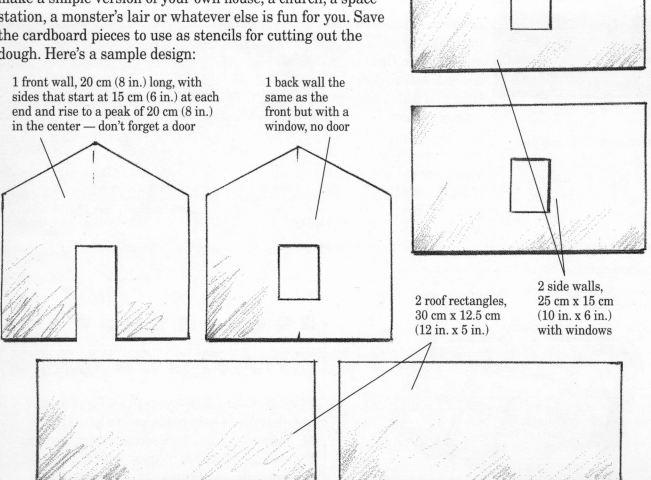

1 front wall, 20 cm (8 in.) long, with
sides that start at 15 cm (6 in.) at each
end and rise to a peak of 20 cm (8 in.)
in the center — don't forget a door

1 back wall the
same as the
front but with a
window, no door

2 roof rectangles,
30 cm x 12.5 cm
(12 in. x 5 in.)

2 side walls,
25 cm x 15 cm
(10 in. x 6 in.)
with windows

MAKING THE DOUGH

Make the dough the day before you cook it.

You'll need:
250 mL (1 cup) butter or margarine
250 mL (1 cup) sugar
250 mL (1 cup) molasses
2 eggs
about 2 L (8 cups) all-purpose flour
15 mL (1 tablespoon) ground cinnamon
10 mL (2 teaspoons) ground cloves
10 mL (2 teaspoons) ground ginger
10 mL (2 teaspoons) baking powder
5 mL (1 teaspoon) nutmeg
5 mL (1 teaspoon) baking soda
waxed paper and plastic wrap
a large bowl and a medium bowl
a fork, a rolling pin and an electric mixer

1.
In a large bowl, beat the butter or margarine until soft.

2.
Add sugar and molasses and beat at high speed until fluffy. Then beat in the two eggs until well mixed.

3.
In a medium bowl, use a fork to mix 1500 mL (6 cups) of the flour and the other dry ingredients.

4.
Beat the dry ingredients into the wet mixture from step 2, 250 mL (1 cup) at a time. Beat until the dough is soft.

5.
Turn the dough onto a floured surface and knead by turning it over and over and pressing down on it with the base of your hands. Add some of the last 250 mL (1 cup) of flour until the dough is no longer sticky but is smooth and easily molded.

6.
Divide the dough into eight pieces. With a rolling pin, flatten each piece into a 20 cm x 15 cm (8 in. x 6 in.) slab. Pile the slabs on top of each other, separated by sheets of waxed paper. Wrap the pile in plastic and refrigerate.

Turn the page for instructions on how to cut out, bake and assemble your gingerbread house.

MORE

BAKING THE GINGERBREAD

1.

Preheat the oven to 180°C (350°F).

2.

With a rolling pin, roll each piece of dough in its waxed paper wrapping until the dough is about 0.5 cm (¼ in.) thick.

3.

Put a little butter on a piece of paper and rub it over a cookie sheet.

4.

Peel the waxed paper off one piece of dough and place the dough on one end of the cookie sheet. Arrange one or more cardboard stencils of the house on the dough and cut them out with a knife. Remove the left-over pieces of dough. Use a spatula to separate the parts of the house, as the dough will enlarge slightly with cooking.

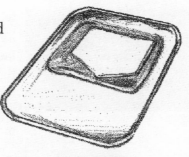

5.

Repeat step 4 with another rectangle of dough on the cookie sheet. When the cookie sheet is full, bake the pieces for about 10 minutes, or until they turn a warm brown color and harden a little around the edges.

6.

Remove the cooked gingerbread with a wide flipper to a wire rack to cool.

7.

Repeat steps 3 to 6 until all the house pieces are cooked.

DECORATOR FROSTING

You'll need:
1¼ L (5½ cups) icing sugar
4 egg whites
2 mL (½ teaspoon) cream of tartar
a large bowl, an electric mixer

1.

In the large bowl, mix the ingredients. Once blended, turn mixer to high and beat for about 5 minutes, or until you can run a knife through the icing and the mark stays.

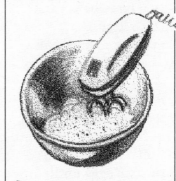

2.

Cover the bowl with plastic wrap so the wrap is pressed right down on the top of the icing. If the icing is exposed to air, it will harden. Refrigerate until needed.

ASSEMBLING AND DECORATING THE HOUSE

You'll need:

125 mL (½ cup) white sugar

decorator frosting (see recipe on page 110)

colorful hard candies such as Life Savers and cake decorations

a frying pan

1.

With an adult's help, spread the white sugar in the frying pan. Heat the sugar slowly, stirring often, until the sugar turns brown and syrupy. Turn the heat to low.

2.

Pick up two walls of the house that meet at a corner and put those ends into the syrup. Press together, holding for a few seconds, until the syrup hardens. Repeat with the other walls until all four hold together and the house stands on its own. Place on the gingerbread base.

3.

Repeat step 2 with the roof pieces. Press the pieces together at the angle that forms the peak on the front and back walls. Place the roof on the house.

4.

Dip a knife in warm water and then into the decorator frosting. Spread the frosting to look like snow on the roof, base and windowsills. Then, press candies into the frosting to make an attractive design.

111

WINTER CAMPFIRE

Follow these directions for a merry and safe outdoor fire. Then you can warm your hands on Olympic Day (see page 120) or during an evening on the rink (see page 48).

- With an adult's help, choose a site away from buildings, trees, woodpiles and overhanging limbs. Take the same precautions as for a summer campfire — a spark can start a dangerous blaze at any time of year. Keep a pail of sand close by for smothering the fire as well as a shovel for scooping snow onto flames or sparks.

- You need three sizes of wood — tinder, kindling and fuel. Collect fallen birchbark, dead twigs, dry pinecones and needles for tinder. And, in the meadow, gather dry dead weeds, including goldenrod, cattails and milkweed stalks sticking out of the snow. For kindling, prune the dead needle-free lower branches off conifers such as spruce, hemlock and pine. Make a stack of dry, split hardwood logs for fuel.

- Form a base for the fire by laying four or five similar-sized whole logs side by side on the snow. Next, make a mound of tinder with a few pieces of kindling on top. Use a long-handled match to light the tinder. When the tinder is burning well, add more kindling, starting with the smaller pieces and adding larger ones as the fire catches. When the fire is burning well, add several pieces of dry firewood. Never leave the fire unattended.

- Keep adding fuel to the bonfire throughout the evening. Before going indoors, douse the fire completely with snow and sand, stirring the embers with a stick until they're cold and there's no smoke.

HOT CHOCOLATE

Bring a Thermos filled with hot chocolate to your campfire, and warm up your insides as well.

You'll need:
15 mL (1 heaping tablespoon) cocoa
5 mL (1 heaping teaspoon) sugar
50 mL (¼ cup) boiling water
250 mL (1 cup) milk
oven mitts
a heavy pot
a wooden spoon
a Thermos with a cup lid

1.
Stir together cocoa, sugar and boiling water in a heavy pot.

2.
Add milk and stir until the mixture begins to boil. Remove from the heat.

3.
Preheat the Thermos with hot water. Pour out. Pour the hot chocolate into the warm Thermos and tighten the lid.

113

SNACKS AND TREATS

Between celebration activities, it's great to have something tasty to crunch on. You may have to make double batches for seconds all round!

POPCORN BRITTLE

You'll need:

125 mL (½ cup) butter or margarine

175 mL (³/₄ cup) brown sugar

50 mL (¼ cup) white corn syrup

2 mL (½ teaspoon) baking soda

2 L (8 cups) popped popcorn

¼ L (1 cup) peanuts (optional)

a pot, a spoon, oven mitts and a baking pan

1.

Preheat the oven to 180°C (350°F).

2.

Melt the butter or margarine in a pot on the stove and then add the brown sugar and corn syrup. Heat the mixture until it comes to a boil. Then, lower the heat and let it simmer for 3 minutes without stirring.

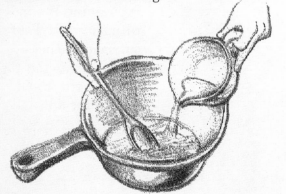

3.

Take the mixture off the stove and stir in baking soda to make it foamy.

4.

Pour the popped popcorn (and peanuts, if you like) onto your baking pan and then cover with the foamy mixture. Stir to coat all the pieces.

5.

Cook 7 to 10 minutes in the oven.

6.

Remove the pan from the oven and let cool. Stir once or twice. When it's cool enough to touch, break the large pieces apart with your hands. Store what you don't eat in a sealed cookie tin or plastic bag.

QUICK AND CHEESY POPCORN

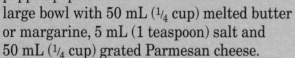

If you have only enough time to make a quick popcorn snack, toss 2 L (8 cups) of popped popcorn in a large bowl with 50 mL (¼ cup) melted butter or margarine, 5 mL (1 teaspoon) salt and 50 mL (¼ cup) grated Parmesan cheese.

NUTS 'N BOLTS

You'll need:

15 mL (1 tablespoon) vegetable oil

250 mL (1 cup) spoon-sized shredded wheat

250 mL (1 cup) toasted "O" cereal, such as Cheerios

2 mL (½ teaspoon) seasoned salt

250 mL (1 cup) short pretzel sticks

175mL (¾ cup) toasted peanuts or soybeans (optional)

a large frying pan, a spoon and a bowl

1.
Pour the vegetable oil into the frying pan and heat at the lowest setting. Add the two cereals and stir until lightly toasted.

2.
Sprinkle with salt.

3.
Remove the frying pan from the heat and add pretzels and peanuts or soybeans.

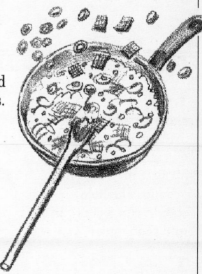

4.
Stir to mix thoroughly and let cool. Pour into a bowl and serve.

115

SUGARING OFF

Where sugar maples grow, there is a sweet time in March when the days warm above freezing but the nights turn sharply cold. That's when the sap starts to run in sugar maple trees. You can collect some of that sap and make maple syrup.

You'll need:

several sugar maple trees that measure more than 100 cm (40 in.) around the trunk at 1 m (3 ft.) from the ground

a hand drill with a 1 cm (½ in.) bit

a hammer

4 spiles or 4 12 cm (4½ in.) lengths of 1 cm (½ in.) copper pipe (you can ask the hardware store to cut it for you)

5 pails

a strainer

a large, heavy pot

oven mitts

a long-handled wooden spoon

a clean jar

pliers

1.

Have an adult help you drill a hole in the trunk of a sugar maple tree about 1 m (3 ft.) off the ground. The hole should run 8 cm (3 in.) into the trunk.

2.

Hammer a spile or copper pipe into the hole. Hang a pail on the spile.

3.

Repeat for each spile. You can insert two spiles per tree as long as they are on opposite sides of the trunk.

116

4.

Collect the sap from your pails each day and pour it through a fine strainer into a storage pail. Store the strained sap in the refrigerator.

5.

When you have collected enough sap to fill a large pot, have an adult help you to heat the sap on top of the stove until it boils. Turn it down to simmer and stir occasionally until most of the water evaporates. This may take all day and should be done in a room with a vent or an open window so the steam can escape.

6.

When you have only a small amount of golden brown syrup in the bottom of the pot, pour it into a clean jar and cool. Turn the page for recipes for enjoying your maple syrup.

7.

Pull the spiles out of the trees with pliers and plug the holes with sticks.

SWEET FEAST

Homemade pancakes covered in fresh maple syrup (see page 116) — can you think of anything better? This recipe makes enough to feed four hungry people.

You'll need:

375 mL (1½ cups) all-purpose flour

5 mL (1 teaspoon) salt

45 ml (3 tablespoons) sugar

10 mL (2 teaspoons) double-acting baking powder

300 mL (1¼ cups) milk

3 eggs, slightly beaten

45 mL (3 tablespoons) melted butter

25 mL (2 tablespoons) vegetable oil or butter for frying

2 large bowls, a fork and a frying pan or griddle

1.

In a large bowl, mix together the flour, salt, baking powder and sugar with a fork.

2.

In another bowl, combine the milk and eggs. Add the butter and stir.

3.

Mix the wet ingredients into the dry ones with a few quick strokes. Don't over beat — leave a few lumps in the batter for lighter pancakes.

4.

Warm up the frying pan or griddle for about 30 seconds over medium-high heat. Add the oil or butter and swirl to cover the surface of the pan.

5.

Ladle 125 mL (½ cup) portions of batter onto the hot surface — they shouldn't touch each other.

6.

After about 3 minutes, or when bubbles appear on the top of the pancakes, turn them with a flipper. Cook the second side for about half as long as the first.

7.

As you make them, pile up the pancakes on a plate in a warm oven. When the last one is cooked, serve at once. Pass the maple syrup around.

MAPLE SUNDAES

Maple syrup is delicious with ice cream. Pour the syrup on top of a scoop of vanilla ice cream in a bowl. Sprinkle with chopped walnuts and place a maraschino cherry on top.

SUGAR MAPLE TAFFY

Pioneers used to boil some of their maple syrup until it was very thick and then they poured it on clean snow. When the syrup started to cool, the kids picked up strands and pulled them as they hardened. Once hard and cold, everyone licked pieces of taffy.

WINTER OLYMPICS

Make the Olympics happen every winter — a special event shared with family and friends. You can count on rosy cheeks, tingling toes and a day of extraordinary fun.

PLANNING AHEAD

- Form a small planning committee with an adult helper.

- Set a date, with an alternate storm date.

- If possible, pick a site that includes a small hill, a flat snowy field or lawn and a place to skate.

- Decide on the number of participants and deliver notices to your neighbors and friends.

- Invite two or more people to act as judges. They'll need stopwatches.

- Make a trophy for the winning team and the runners-up that can be used each year. Make or buy funny prizes for the other participants.

- Set up a "refueling booth" with hot chocolate (see page 113) and snacks (see page 114).

- Plan for and lay an outdoor fire, if you like (see page 112).

CHOOSING TEAMS

Avoid hurt feelings on the big day by dividing the group ahead of time into two fair teams with two team leaders. Make sure each team has members from all age groups.

Using two different colors of felt, make badges or ribbons for all members of each team. Name your team after your family or favorite animal, such as the Wolverines versus the Grizzlies. When the teams assemble on Olympic Day, team leaders welcome each player and pin badges on their jackets.

CHOOSING EVENTS

Olympic Day should include group events for people of all ages as well as individual challenges. For each hour of competition, you'll need three or more events. Decide ahead of time how points will be scored and recorded. Try the following suggestions, make up your own wacky additions to the fun and check out other possibilities from this book:

Snow soccer, page 42;
Snow snake, page 46;
Rink games, page 50;
Snowshoeing, page 55;
Cross-country skiing, page 56.

MORE

121

ON THE SLOPES

Who can toboggan or ski down the hill the fastest? If that's too ordinary, try some of these zany team challenges and dream up your own, too. Before the games begin, make sure an adult checks the hill for rocks and other hazards hiding in the snow. Wear a helmet on steep slopes.

ROLL RACE

Toss a coin to see which team goes first. At the top of the hill, five members from the first team lie down in a line holding onto the ankles of the next person. Record how long it takes for them to roll to the bottom of the hill. Then time the second team. The fastest team wins.

TOBOGGAN RACE

At the top of the hill, teams are given identical cardboard boxes. The judge says "go!" and each team quickly designs and makes a toboggan. The player on each team whose birthday is closest to Olympic Day slides down the hill and runs the toboggan back up to the next player. All team members must slide down the path made by the first player. The team that finishes first wins.

LUGE RUN

If the snow and temperature conditions are right, the grooves made by the cardboard toboggans will become icy, just like an Olympic luge run. With an adult supervising, try sliding down the run on your bottom.

WACKY RELAY

Teams choose four members. Two go to the top of the hill, two to the bottom. Beginning at the bottom, one player from each team runs backward up the hill singing loudly and high-fives a waiting teammate. She sits on her bottom and, making a rowing motion with her arms, propels herself down the hill. High fives again. The third player hops on one foot up the hill, clapping his hands. High fives again. The last player somersaults down to finish. Which team came first? High fives all round.

SNOWY RELAY

Gather both teams at the top of the hill, each equipped with a small pail. When the judge says "go," the first member of each team takes the pail, runs to the bottom of the hill, fills it with snow, runs back uphill and dumps out the pail of snow. Continue until all members of the teams have had a turn. The judge decides which team has the biggest pile of snow. Now see which team can make the biggest snowman.

MORE

BULKY JUMPING

The long jump or hop-step-jump are a breeze in shorts and a T-shirt, right? See how far you can jump wearing your own outerwear plus the biggest adult snowsuit, mitts and boots available.

- Each team has five participants for each jump.

- Take turns jumping wearing the extra clothing.

- The judge records the jump lengths and determines the winning team.

RUNNING RACES

Running through snow can be difficult and hilarious at the same time. Using the following instructions, try these races: straight running, three-legged, wheelbarrow and running backward. Whew!

- Set up a snowy running track about 50 m (55 yd.) in length. Make a start and finish line with a string strung between two ski poles or hockey sticks stuck in the snow.

- Run the races in heats with different age groups — such as 4 to 7, 8 to 11, 12 to 16, 17 to 20, 21 and over.

- One judge starts the races and the other decides the winners.

CHALLENGES ON ICE

Make clearing the ice part of the games. Divide the ice surface in half. Provide each team with one shovel and see which team can clear its half the fastest.

SPEED SKATING RELAY

With one arm behind his back and the other arm swinging in a steady rhythm, the skater swoops around the circuit at breathtaking speed. Is it the bathing cap that makes him skate so fast? You'll need two bathing caps, four boots and an equal number of players from each team for this event.

- Place a boot 2 m (6½ ft.) from each corner of the rink.

- Players line up behind their team leader. Leaders put on bathing caps.

- The judge says "go." Staying outside the boot markers, one player from each team skates once around the rink and passes the bathing cap on to his waiting teammate.

- Continue until all members of the teams have had a turn. The winning team finishes first.

CLOSING CEREMONIES

Add up the points from each event to find a winning team. The team leaders make speeches and give out prizes. Make sure all participants are included. Award a crazy prize to the Olympian who:

- drank the most hot chocolate

- had the reddest nose

- made everyone laugh

- had the most snow in her boots

INDEX